OXFORD WORLD'S CLASSICS

*For over 100 years Oxford World's Classics have brought
readers closer to the world's great literature. Now with over 700
titles—from the 4,000-year-old myths of Mesopotamia to the
twentieth century's greatest novels—the series makes available
lesser-known as well as celebrated writing.*

*The pocket-sized hardbacks of the early years contained
introductions by Virginia Woolf, T. S. Eliot, Graham Greene,
and other literary figures which enriched the experience of reading.
Today the series is recognized for its fine scholarship and
reliability in texts that span world literature, drama and poetry,
religion, philosophy and politics. Each edition includes perceptive
commentary and essential background information to meet the
changing needs of readers.*

OXFORD WORLD'S CLASSICS

====

JOHN SUTHERLAND

So You Think You Know Thomas Hardy?

A Literary Quizbook

====

OXFORD

UNIVERSITY PRESS

OXFORD
UNIVERSITY PRESS

Great Clarendon Street, Oxford OX2 6DP

Oxford University Press is a department of the University of Oxford.
It furthers the University's objective of excellence in research, scholarship,
and education by publishing worldwide in

Oxford New York

Auckland Cape Town Dar es Salaam Hong Kong Karachi
Kuala Lumpur Madrid Melbourne Mexico City Nairobi
New Delhi Shanghai Taipei Toronto

With offices in

Argentina Austria Brazil Chile Czech Republic France Greece
Guatemala Hungary Italy Japan Poland Portugal Singapore
South Korea Switzerland Thailand Turkey Ukraine Vietnam

Oxford is a registered trade mark of Oxford University Press
in the UK and in certain other countries

Published in the United States
by Oxford University Press Inc., New York

© John Sutherland 2005

British Library Cataloguing in Publication Data

Data available

Library of Congress Cataloging in Publication Data

Data available

Typeset in Ehrhardt
by RefineCatch Limited, Bungay, Suffolk
Printed in Great Britain by
Clays Ltd, St Ives plc

ISBN 0–19–280443–X   978–0–19–280443–3

CONTENTS

INTRODUCTION

There are two ways of existing for ever, as a living creature
or as a mummy. Now in these days of literary activity the
continuation of a large number of literary mummies is
certain. They will be preserved in their hundreds by bio-
graphies, dictionaries, etc. We shall know their names, but
how many writers of the Victorian era will remain alive
through the ages? Half a dozen?

Maarten Maartens, 1889

Alas, Maarten Maartens, a well-regarded novelist and a contemporary
(1858–1915) of Thomas Hardy's, has joined the mummies. Hardy is
one of the half-dozen or so novelists of the Victorian period who still
'lives'—along with Charles Dickens, George Eliot, William Makepeace
Thackeray, Charlotte and Emily Brontë, and Anthony Trollope. These
writers' major works sell, in the twenty-first century, even more
strongly than they did in the nineteenth. Their novels are adapted for
large and small screen for audiences of millions magnitudes larger
than anything Maartens could have imagined.

Oxford University Press has, through its World's Classics and
Oxford World's Classics series, served this golden nucleus with
admirably annotated, handsomely produced, budget-priced texts.
OUP has also published Michael Millgate's definitive *Thomas Hardy:
A Biography* (1985; rev. ed. 2004), Simon Gatrell's *Hardy the Creator:
A Textual Biography* (1988), Michael Millgate and Richard Purdy's
seven-volume set of Hardy's *Collected Letters* (1978–88), and Norman
Page's invaluable *Oxford Reader's Companion to Hardy* (2000), together
with many critical monographs on the fiction and poetry.

So You Think You Know Thomas Hardy? is designed to fill a small
crevice in this impressive scholarly pile. As with its predecessor, *So
You Think You Know Jane Austen?*, the book is derived from a teaching
method which I call 'Quiz and Questionnaire'. Essentially, it means
approaching the text of a novel from two directions. The first assesses
what one, as reader, knows factually (along the lines of 'How old is
Tess Clare, née Durbeyfield, when she is hanged?'). How well do you
know, or remember, the narrative? The quiz will tell.

The second approach tests what one knows—or can plausibly construct—by deduction and hypothesis ('Is Tess pregnant at the time of her execution?'). I have added to the mixture a few queries and quibbles and some interpretative problems. How deep can you get into the novel? Can you 'feel', seismographically, what is happening in the background but not narrated? The immediate pay-off from applying this two-pronged method to fiction like Hardy's (or Austen's) is that he loads his stories with what Henry James called 'solidity of specification'. We can legitimately ask real-world questions of realistic fiction.

The argument in favour of Q & Q is, I would contend, twofold: it's a pleasing way to read and, whatever its critical simple-mindedness, it brings the reader close to the text. The basic contention, underlying the exercise, is simple: the best way to read Thomas Hardy is to read Thomas Hardy. Carefully.

Six 'Wessex' Novels (of Hardy's fourteen-strong oeuvre) are covered in chronological order of publication. They are the titles which are most frequently written about by critics, set for examination and adapted for film, television, and radio. One might go further to say they are the most loved of Hardy's novels and, deservedly, those to which readers most regularly return—and will, as Maarten Maartens predicted, 'for ages'.

Dale Kramer, an expert Hardy scholar and Oxford World's Classics editor, has been most helpful in correcting details, generally commenting, and making valuable suggestions. All error that remains is, however, attributable to JS.

THE QUIZZES

A Note on the Quizzes

There follow four tests—of graduated difficulty. The first ('**Level One: Brass Tacks**') contains straightforwardly factual questions which admit of direct, unequivocal answers. The second test ('**Level Two: Factual but Tricky**') contains a more demanding set of questions of basically the same kind. The next test ('**Level Three: Very Tricky and Occasionally Deductive**') is approaching mastermind difficulty in terms of factual reference and involves some interpretive deduction as well. The Fourth Test ('**Level Four: The Interpretative Zone**') invites deduction and speculation.

The answers, following the italicized questions, will be found at the end of the book. Readers wishing merely to think about Hardy's fiction and not be pestered by owlish questions may go straight to the second section.

Far from the Madding Crowd

Introductory Note on the Novel

Far from the Madding Crowd was Hardy's fourth published novel, and the work with which he ascended to mass popularity with the Victorian reading public. The work was commissioned as a serial by Leslie Stephen, the editor of the country's premier magazine, the *Cornhill*, in whose pages it appeared monthly between January and December 1874, illustrated by H. Allingham. As it came to the end of its serial run, the novel was published in two volumes, for the library market, by Smith, Elder & Co. (*Cornhill*'s publisher). It was a momentous year for the novelist. In 1874 he married his first wife, Emma Lavinia. The marriage would prove to be difficult. There were no children. When the novel was a third written, Hardy's closest friend, Horace Moule, cut his throat in his rooms at Cambridge. The event cast a shadow over the later portions of Hardy's narrative and probably over his whole later life. In addition to winning him fame, *Far from the Madding Crowd* also attracted the kind of censorious criticism which would follow Hardy for the remainder of his novel-writing career and eventually drive him out of the field altogether. Readers particularly objected to the Fanny Robin subplot. None the less, *Far from the Madding Crowd* set expectations for Hardy that lasted during his lifetime. Subsequent title pages often bore the notice 'By the Author of *Far from the Madding Crowd*'. His later novels were routinely compared to it (often unfavourably).

Level One: Brass Tacks

1/1 With what description does the novel begin?

1/2 What are the (ominous) colours which strike the watching Gabriel's eye, when he first observes Bathsheba, perched on all her worldly goods, trundling up Norcombe Hill?

1/3 What is the name of the cow who is the occasion of Oak's second meeting with Bathsheba?

1/4 Like 'Mary' in the nursery rhyme, Bathsheba, it seems (thanks to Gabriel), will have 'a little [nameless] lamb' to follow her, 'wherever she goes'. Does this lamb (like George the dog, Daisy the cow, and Poppet the mare) have any afterlife in the narrative?

1/5 What is Gabriel's first feeling, and what his first exclamation, on losing the whole of his flock?

1/6 What are Gabriel's first words to Bathsheba, after his offer of marriage is declined?

1/7 Why is 'Henery' Fray so called, and not 'Henry'?

1/8 What is Joseph Poorgrass's great 'defect'?

1/9 For whom did Bathsheba originally intend the valentine which eventually (with the fatal seal 'Marry Me') is sent to Boldwood?

1/10 What is the 'instrument of salvation' with which Gabriel saves forty-nine of Bathsheba's bloated flock?

1/11 What, according to the maltster, Smallbury, is the true test of being 'an old man worth naming'?

1/12 What is Troy's motto, in his treatment of women?

1/13 What are the names of Bathsheba's three female attendants?

1/14 Which are the two horses used for the Troy–Everdene gig; and which of the married couple prefers which?

1/15 What is Troy's signal to Bathsheba that he has secretly arrived at the farm?

1/16 What is the chalk inscription on the lid of Fanny's coffin? How does Gabriel change it? And why?

1/17 What is Bathsheba's initial reaction to what she discovers in Fanny's coffin, when she breaks it open?

1/18 What is Bathsheba's immediate reaction when her husband kisses Fanny in her coffin?

1/19 How is Troy saved from drowning?

1/20 What profession does Troy go in for in the United States?

1/21 What profession does Troy go in for on his return to England?

1/22 Who sees through Troy's Turpin disguise at the funfair?

1/23 What is Joseph Poorgrass's 'old complaint'?

1/24 How long is Troy away, presumed drowned?

1/25 What is Boldwood's response, on being foiled in his attempt to kill himself?

☞ *Check answers at the back of the volume. If you scored over 15, proceed to Level Two ('Factual but Tricky'). If*

*you scored over 10 but under 15, skim the novel again.
Over 5 but under 10, reread the novel. Under 5, throw
this book away and watch TV.*

Level Two: Factual but Tricky

2/1 Gabriel first meets Bathsheba on the toll-road, as she is moving all her worldly goods to her aunt's cottage, near Norcombe Hill. He pays the toll which she has disputed, regarding it as excessively expensive. Before the encounter with the gatekeeper, out of his sight (but seen by Gabriel), the young woman admires herself in a 'small swing looking-glass'. After she has passed by, the two men agree she is a 'handsome maid' but concur that she has a 'great fault'. What is it?

2/2 What is the occasion of Oak's second personal encounter with Bathsheba?

2/3 Why does Oak dread 'the eighth day'?

2/4 What, as the narrative jestingly puts it, does Oak's hair look like as he makes himself presentable to bring a lamb and (thereafter) offer marriage to Bathsheba?

2/5 The narrative informs us that 'Farmer Oak had one-and-a-half Christian characteristics too many to succeed with Bathsheba'. What are these 'characteristics'?

2/6 The high point in Gabriel's career is his final union with the heiress, and his one-and-only love, Bathsheba. What is the lowest point in his career?

2/7 What is the great communal beer mug at Warren's Malthouse called, and why?

2/8 Who is the fattest and who the thinnest among the company at Warren's Malthouse?

2/9 What are the two novels we know Oak has read?

2/10 How did Cain Ball come by his sinister (un-)Christian name?

2/11 What characteristic 'pre-eminently' marks Farmer Boldwood?

2/12 How does Liddy suggest that Bathsheba find out if she will ever marry, and what is the result?

2/13 What is the name of Boldwood's farm?

2/14 How long does it take Oak to shear a sheep?

2/15 Who is the first person ever to kiss Bathsheba, and how old is she at the time?

2/16 Who, or what kind of person, glides through the night as silently as a woman can?

2/17 What happy misfortune allowed Joseph Poorgrass to read *The Pilgrim's Progress*?

2/18 What is an 'Early Ball'?

2/19 What tipple does Troy prefer to the local ale and mead, and with what does he fuddle the farmworkers at the Harvest Supper?

2/20 What are the only examples we are given of Troy's 'romanticism'?

2/21 What (insofar as the reader is informed) is signally missing on the inscription which Troy ordains for Fanny's gravestone, 'Erected by Francis Troy in Beloved Memory of Fanny Robin'?

2/22 What change of events brings Gabriel to be bailiff, or steward, of both the Upper and Lower Weatherbury farms?

2/23 What is written in the note which Pennyways slips Bathsheba at the fair, and which Troy ingeniously steals before she can read it?

2/24 What reason does Bathsheba give Gabriel for finally accepting the marriage proposal of Boldwood?

2/25 How old is Troy when he dies?

☞ *Answers at the back of the book. Anything over 12 is good, indicating either strong memory or recent acquaintance. Go on to Level Three ('Very Tricky—and Occasionally Deductive') which requires, in addition to intimate knowledge of the text, an ability to make plausible deductions from it.*

Level Three: Very Tricky—and Occasionally Deductive

3/1 Bathsheba saves Gabriel's life, in his hut, as it fills up with poisonous carbon monoxide. Why does she venture into his dwelling place, closed as the doors and the two small windows are?

3/2 Why, after her aunt (perhaps with Bathsheba's acquiescence) has sent the wooer Gabriel away (with the falsehood that her niece has other, more eligible suitors), does the young lady chase after him?

3/3 Hardy includes 'The Mistake' as part of the title for the chapter (4) in which Gabriel makes his marriage offer to Bathsheba. Are we to take the title as meaning 'It is a mistake on Gabriel's part to think of marrying such a "vain" woman'? Or, 'Bathsheba is at pains to correct the mistaken impression given by her aunt that she has a troop of other lovers'? Or, 'Bathsheba's biggest mistake in life is not to marry the man who so faithfully loves her when he first asks'?

3/4 How does Gabriel meet Fanny Robin, and how does he discover the story of her love entanglement?

3/5 Does anyone realize that the valentine sent to Boldwood has the dangerous motto, 'Marry Me', engraved on its sealing wax?

3/6 Who, might one plausibly suggest, is the first dyslexic to be described in English fiction?

3/7 What fateful error does Fanny Robin make about the barracks-town church in which she is to be married?

3/8 What ballad does Bathsheba sing at the shearing-supper, and why is it 'remembered for many months, and even years'?

3/9 What love token does Troy, impulsively, give to Bathsheba when he scarcely knows her?

3/10 Troy's display of swordsmanship to Bathsheba is almost too obviously phallic. With what examples of virtuosity does he crown his display?

3/11 Troy tells Bathsheba (falsely, as Oak easily discovers) that he attends church at Weatherbury secretly, entering by the back tower door, and remaining during the service unseen. Why would he do this, and how, plausibly, could he explain to Bathsheba (infatuated as she is) his motive for doing so?

3/12 To what does Bathsheba attribute her lack of 'capacity for love'?

3/13 Instead of returning to his 'distant barracks', as Boldwood hopes, Troy (in the period immediately before his marriage) goes to Bath, 'to visit some acquaintance'. Is there anything to be known about what he does in Bath, in these tense few days?

3/14 Who is the parson at Weatherbury, and what do we know of him?

3/15 What reason does Troy give Boldwood for leaving the army?

3/16 What happens to the dog, a canine Good Samaritan, which brings Fanny to the Workhouse?

3/17 How does Fanny's corpse end up in an inn?

3/18 After her terrible, and final, quarrel with Troy, Bathsheba locks herself in an attic. She asks Liddy to bring her books. What, particularly?

3/19 What misadventure befalls Fanny's grave—unlucky in death as she is in life?

3/20 Susan Tall, the termagant wife, notes that the former shepherd's garb has changed with his promotion to bailiff status. How, exactly?

3/21 Chapter 50 opens: 'Greenhill was the Nijnii Novgorod of South Wessex'. Is this a helpful comparison?

3/22 Who is it that prevents Boldwood from turning the second barrel of his shotgun on himself?

3/23 What is the nature of the mortal wound that Troy receives?

3/24 What is Gabriel's first plan, after the murder of Troy?

3/25 What is Gabriel's second plan?

☞ *Answers at the back of the book. The factual questions are very difficult, and some of the questions involve interpretation. If you score anything over 10, go forward to Level Four ('The Interpretative Zone'). If your deductive answers genuinely strike you as more convincing, or ingenious, than mine, give yourself a bonus point (or more).*

Level Four: The Interpretative Zone

4/1 Why 'Wessex'?

4/2 Does Farmer Oak have a grandfather clock?

4/3 What do we know of Farmer Oak's family and background?

4/4 There are often overtones in the characters' names in *Far from the Madding Crowd* ('Oak' is English, of ancient stock, and the strongest of trees, for example). What are the overtones of 'Bathsheba'?

4/5 When a ride over to Tewnell Mill, for oatmeal for Daisy's calf, is necessary, Bathsheba's aunt objects 'there's no side saddle' (in the stable, she means: the women of the household have not ridden before her niece's arrival). Bathsheba replies: 'I can ride on the other [i.e. a man's saddle]: trust me.' What do we deduce from this?

4/6 Why *does* Bathsheba's aunt lie to Gabriel, about her niece's 'many lovers'?

4/7 What do we know of Bathsheba's background, how she came to be so named, how orphaned, and how she came to be, if not rich, prosperous?

4/8 What can we put together of the career and background of Frank Troy?

4/9 Why is Sergeant Troy—educated, brave, and able—no more than a non-commissioned officer?

4/10 Shepherd Oak can speak respectable 'RP' (Received Pronunciation)—'Queen's English'. He also, on occasion, lapses into Wessex dialect. What circumstances condition his speech?

4/11 How many animals does Gabriel kill or injure in the course of the narrative?

4/12 What is Bathsheba doing when she first meets Troy, and how does it happen?

4/13 The cuts, parries, and thrusts of infantrymen, Troy concedes, 'are more interesting than ours', but they lack something that dragoon swordplay has. What?

4/14 What do the numbers 249, 8, 27, and 750 signify in *Far From the Madding Crowd*?

4/15 Liddy obviously knows that Troy is a 'fast' man, and her knowing it causes a rift between her and Bathsheba. Does Liddy really not know of the affair between Fanny and Troy?

4/16 How badly, or intentionally badly, does Troy treat Fanny?

4/17 Does insanity run in Boldwood's family? asks Troy (perhaps rather nervously). Does it?

4/18 What omens, or portents, indicate to Gabriel that a terrible summer storm is on its way?

4/19 Troy gives a very special watch to Bathsheba. Does he have another watch when he does so, and is there anything special about it?

4/20 How is it that Bathsheba does not know that Fanny, one of her servants, has blond hair?

4/21 Liddy Smallbury tells Boldwood that Bathsheba has said 'she might marry again at the end of seven years from last year'. Did Bathsheba say this, and did she (assuming that Liddy is her accomplice) mean it as yet another coquettish signal to the demented Boldwood?

4/22 Why does Troy choose to burst into Boldwood's Christmas party, heavily cloaked?

4/23 What is discovered in the locked closet in Boldwood's house?

4/24 Does Gabriel, finally, propose to Bathsheba, or she to him?

4/25 Do Gabriel and Bathsheba have, as she demands, 'the most private, secret, plainest wedding that it is possible to have'?

☞ *Check answers at the end of the book. Give yourself a bonus for every interpretative answer which seems to you (1) correct (2) more plausible, witty, or ingenious than that which I offer.*

   Total all your marks. If you scored 100 (or more), write your own book. Over 60, congratulations; 30 or less—you will have the pleasure of rereading **Far from the Madding Crowd**.

The Return of the Native

Introductory Note on the Novel

With this novel Hardy returned to the Wessex setting which he had temporarily abandoned with *The Hand of Ethelberta* (1876). He was by now well known in London literary circles and widely regarded as one of the country's major novelists. *The Return of the Native* was serialized in the monthly magazine *Belgravia* (then owned by Chatto & Windus), January–December 1878, with illustrations by Arthur Hopkins, and published in three volumes, for the library market, by Smith, Elder & Co. in late 1878. Hardy affixed a map of 'Wessex' for the book edition. During a restless phase of his life (before his own final 'return' to the Dorchester area) Hardy composed the novel while resident at Sturminster Newton. As a somewhat indignant footnote records, Hardy was prevailed upon by the magazine editor to supply the 'happy' ending with its marriage of Diggory and Thomasin.

Level One: Brass Tacks

1/1 The first section of the narrative is entitled 'The Three Women'. Who are they?

1/2 Diggory Venn has a 'van'. What draws it?

1/3 Who is the man 'no woman will marry'?

1/4 What, according to Grandfer Cantle, is the sole thing that can be said against mead (fermented honey drink)?

1/5 What is Eustacia's 'great desire'?

1/6 Where do Wildeve and Eustacia have their outdoor rendezvous?

1/7 Which of his favourite apples does Thomasin select for Clym?

1/8 What play do the Egdon mummers put on for Christmas?

1/9 What is Clym's birth name?

1/10 What is the name of the inn at which much of the action takes place?

1/11 When do the peasantry have their hair cut?

1/12 What dowry does Mrs Yeobright have to give Thomasin?

1/13 How much does Clym discover a furze–cutter earns?

1/14 What excuse does Wildeve give his wife for his going to East Egdon, where he knows there will be a dance and, probably, Eustacia to dance with?

1/15 What is the signal which, in summers past, Wildeve used to announce his presence outside the house to Eustacia, so as not to arouse the suspicions of her grandfather?

1/16 Which pool is dry in the heat of summer, and which still deep with drinkable water?

1/17 Do Clym and Eustacia have a servant in their house at Alderworth?

1/18 To what does Christian Cantle liken the eye of an adder?

1/19 What, late in the action, do we learn is yet another signal that Wildeve uses to announce—furtively—that he is in the area and has come to see Eustacia?

1/20 What, as we know them, are Eustacia's last words? And what Wildeve's?

1/21 What curse does Susan, as she destroys the effigy of Eustacia, utter?

1/22 Where do Thomasin and little Eustacia finally make their home?

1/23 What colour coat does the whitened Diggory appear in, when he introduces himself to the widowed Thomasin?

1/24 How does Diggory indicate to Thomasin that he is presenting himself to her as a suitor?

1/25 What souvenir of Eustacia does Clym give the faithful Charley?

☞ *Check answers at the back of the volume. If you scored over 15, proceed to Level Two ('Factual but Tricky'). If you scored over 10 but under 15, skim the novel again. Over 5 but under 10, reread the novel. Under 5, throw this book away and watch TV.*

Level Two: Factual but Tricky

2/1 What is the pace of life in the Egdon valleys?

2/2 Who is the native who returns?

2/3 When and where did Grandfer Cantle enlist as a soldier?

2/4 Why could the marriage between Damon and Thomasin not take place?

2/5 What, to his dismay, does Captain Drew discover that his granddaughter, Eustacia, has used for her bonfire?

2/6 What is peculiar about Eustacia's eyes?

2/7 What is Eustacia's reply to Wildeve's suggestion that they emigrate, instantly, to Wisconsin?

2/8 What dream does Eustacia have, on the night of Clym's return, and how does it end?

2/9 In return for allowing her to take his part in the mummers' play, what does young Charley demand, and what does he get from Eustacia?

2/10 Who 'gives Thomasin away' at her (second) wedding to Wildeve?

2/11 What is the difference between a furze-cutter and a heath-cropper?

2/12 How does Susan Nunsuch counteract Eustacia's 'bewitching' of Susan's son (as she thinks)?

2/13 Which is the only season when Eustacia can bear the 'heath'?

2/14 Who says (as many could in Hardy's fiction) 'I am wrongly made'?

2/15 What do Christian and Wildeve use for a gaming table, and what do Wildeve and Venn use for light when the second dice game is played?

2/16 What, according to the Southerton surgeon, has caused Clym's eye problems?

2/17 What is it that finally prostrates Mrs Yeobright on her epic hike back from Alderworth to Blooms-End?

2/18 What medicine do the residents of Blooms-End cottages apply to the wound of Mrs Yeobright?

2/19 What does Wildeve propose to do with his windfall?

2/20 Who is it that discloses that it was probably as much a broken heart as an adder sting which killed Mrs Yeobright?

2/21 Who chooses the Wildeves' baby's name, Eustacia Clementine?

2/22 Thomasin follows Wildeve, as he goes mysteriously onto Egdon, on Guy Fawkes night. As he comes to a fork in the road, what does she overhear him say?

2/23 What is the name of Thomasin's nurse and what is the last thing we see her doing?

2/24 How many dairy cattle does Diggory's dairy have at the end of the novel?

2/25 What are the three activities 'alive' in the widowed and orphaned Clym?

☞ *Answers at the back of the book. Anything over 12 is good, indicating either strong memory or recent acquaintance. Go on to Level Three ('Very Tricky—and Occasionally Deductive') which requires, in addition to intimate knowledge of the text, an ability to make plausible deductions from it.*

Level Three: Very Tricky—and Occasionally Deductive

3/1 In his opening chapter, Hardy uses the terms 'heath' and 'moor' for his wild setting. What, if any, is the difference?

3/2 Why do farmers need 'redding' for their sheep?

3/3 What is the point of the 'festival pyre' which illuminates so vividly the early section of the novel?

3/4 What is the value of the furze that the 'furze cutters' so laboriously gather in? What is the dried weed and shrub used for?

3/5 What is indicated by the various 'braidings' of Thomasin's hair?

3/6 How did Clym become a jewel merchant in Paris?

3/7 What is the second 'wound' Eustacia receives on the Sunday on which she is 'pricked' for a witch?

3/8 What, when not mumming, is Charley's occupation?

3/9 What is the first, ominous, gift which Clym gives Eustacia?

3/10 Who 'might have been called the Rousseau of Egdon'?

3/11 Who is the first person Eustacia ever loved with all her heart?

3/12 What reason does Wildeve give for Thomasin not herself walking across all the way to collect the fifty guineas Mrs Yeobright has for her?

3/13 What ominous error arises from the dice game between Venn and Wildeve?

3/14 Where and what is the 'gypsying'?

3/15 Does Wildeve report Venn's firearm assault on him to the police?

3/16 What does Venn call his campaign against Wildeve?

3/17 Who tells Eustacia about Wildeve's inheriting £11,000, and where does the fortune come from?

3/18 Why, if he knew at the time, did Wildeve not tell Eustacia he was unexpectedly rich, from his uncle's windfall, when he visited her cottage?

3/19 Would Clym have had his nervous collapse had he not been under the 'misapprehension' that it was he, the bad son, who was responsible for his mother's death, by two months' coldness towards the old lady?

3/20 We are told that Thomasin's arrival in Clym's room, in his extremity of self-flagellating remorse, 'came to a sufferer like fresh air into a Black Hole'. What are the implications of the term?

3/21 Why is Wildeve said to be 'twanky'?

3/22 What is the flaw in Eustacia's wild plan to get to Budmouth, then to take a steamer across the channel, and then Paris?

3/23 In his first published version of the narrative, Hardy has Wildeve intend to elope with Eustacia and abandon Thomasin. In his revised version, Wildeve is made to behave more nobly— merely assisting Eustacia's flight with the intention of then returning to his wife. Does Hardy, in the revised version, leave any ambiguity in Wildeve's (reformed) resolution?

3/24 What happens to Johnny Nunsuch after the death of Eustacia, the witch his mother believes (to the point of killing Eustacia in effigy) is responsible for his illness? Does he recover?

3/25 Is Clym a successful itinerant preacher?

☞ *Answers at the back of the book. The factual questions are very difficult, and some of the questions involve interpretation. If you score anything over 10, go forward to Level Four ('The Interpretative Zone'). If your deductive answers genuinely strike you as more convincing, or ingenious, than mine, give yourself a bonus point (or more).*

Level Four: The Interpretative Zone

4/1 In his 1895 Preface, Hardy writes: 'The date at which the following events are assumed to have occurred may be set down as between 1840 and 1850.' Why this antedating of a narrative published in the 1870s?

4/2 Why did Mrs Yeobright 'forbid the banns'?

4/3 What was Diggory's father, and how is it the son finds himself a reddleman?

4/4 What do we know about Wildeve's professional past?

4/5 What do we know of Eustacia's past, and what has brought 'a woman of this sort' to Egdon Heath?

4/6 Why does Captain Drew oppose the lower orders going to school?

4/7 What, as he tells Eustacia, has so 'depressed' Clym?

4/8 Why, after their route to the altar has been so fraught, does Thomasin finally agree to marry Wildeve? Why, on his part (having been lukewarm or fickle hitherto), does he want—precipitately—to tie the knot? Why does Mrs Yeobright, who has never approved, go along with a hugger-mugger union, 'the day after to-morrow'?

4/9 Why does Clym 'return'?

4/10 Why does Clym think he is qualified to run a day school for children and a night school for adults? Why does he give up the worthy line of work he is trained for?

4/11 What is Clym's (wholly misconceived) justification for marrying Eustacia, and what is hers (equally misconceived) for marrying him?

4/12 How many weddings does Mrs Yeobright *not* attend in the narrative?

4/13 Why, given his abilities, does Clym descend to the humble role of furze-cutter?

4/14 When Diggory discharges his gun at Wildeve, as he loiters with lustful intent around Mistover, does the reddleman intend to wound or kill Damon?

4/15 When Clym, the 'native', tells his wife that had he never 'returned' the destinies of three people would have been very different (meaning himself, herself, and his mother), what does Eustacia think?

4/16 Does Wildeve intend seduction when he visits Eustacia by night and by day?

4/17 Is it likely that Mrs Yeobright, although she has never been to her son's house at Alderworth, would not know (even roughly) where it was located (about five miles away; easy walking distance)? Or that, having lived on and by it all her long life, she would get so hopelessly lost, in daylight, on the heath?

4/18 Why did Eustacia not open the door to her mother-in-law, a cruelty from which so much suffering subsequently springs?

4/19 What is Tamsie's 'illness' as she calls it talking to her cousin Clym?

4/20 Where has Diggory Venn been on his long stay away— during which the crisis between the Yeobrights happens?

4/21 Why does Susan Nunsuch firmly believe that Eustacia is a witch?

4/22 It is Johnny Nunsuch who tells Clym the terrible truth of what happened when his mother came to Alderworth. Are there any dubious aspects to Johnny's testimony?

4/23 When he ransacks Eustacia's writing desk, Clym finds nothing incriminating except an empty envelope 'directed to her and the handwriting was Wildeve's'. How does he know Wildeve's handwriting, having been away from the area for so long?

4/24 In justification for her behaviour as a wife, Eustacia tells her infuriated husband (who has discovered the truth of the locked door, as he thinks), 'All persons of refinement have been scared away from me since I sank into the mire of marriage.' Whom is she thinking of?

4/25 Why does Hardy show us so little of the married life of Thomasin and Damon?

☞ *Check answers at the end of the book. Give yourself a bonus for every interpretative answer which seems to you (1) correct (2) more plausible, witty, or ingenious than that which I offer.*

Total all your marks. If you scored 100 (or more), write your own book. Over 60, congratulations; 30 or less— you will have the pleasure of rereading **The Return of the Native.**

The Mayor of Casterbridge

Introductory Note on the Novel

The Mayor of Casterbridge was serialized in the *Graphic*, January–May 1886, with illustrations by Robert Barnes. It was published the same year in two volumes by Smith, Elder & Co. By this stage of his career, Hardy was chafing against the restraints imposed on him, as an artist, by the exigencies of newspaper serialization (profitable as such outlets were for him). He complained that issuing *The Mayor of Casterbridge* in short instalments had required him to over-pack it with incident. It was not until Osgood, McIlvaine & Co.'s 'Wessex Edition' of 1895 that he had the novel in a form of which he could approve. The writing and publication of the novel coincided with Hardy and his wife moving to Max Gate, the house he designed (and his brother built) on the outskirts of Dorchester (i.e. Casterbridge). Hardy's ambivalence about the town in whose environs he would spend the remainder of his long life is reflected in the novel.

Level One: Brass Tacks

1/1 What, in his Preface to the novel, does Hardy identify as the principal event determining the nineteenth-century history of his native region, 'Wessex'?

1/2 When does the action open?

1/3 How old is Henchard, when he makes his great oath, and how old is he when he is reunited with his family?

1/4 At which season of the year do Susan and Elizabeth-Jane return to Weydon Priors?

1/5 What is Henchard's dental state in middle age?

1/6 How long has the regenerate Henchard been sober when Susan sees him again?

1/7 How does Elizabeth-Jane help pay the bill at the Three Mariners?

1/8 Where is Farfrae bound for?

1/9 What refreshment does Henchard offer Farfrae, having hired him?

1/10 What decoratively classical figures flank Henchard's mantelpiece?

1/11 What is Susan's nickname among the children of the town?

1/12 What are Lucetta's various names?

1/13 What was Lucetta's father, by profession, and what kind of childhood did she have?

1/14 Who says, 'the romance of the sower is gone for good'?

1/15 What is 'Mr Fall', the astrologer, called behind his back?

1/16 How much does Henchard pay his waggoners?

1/17 Who is the Mayor of Casterbridge, between Henchard's and Farfrae's terms?

1/18 How did Elizabeth-Jane acquire her 'wonderful skill in netting'?

1/19 Where does Henchard make his home, after his bankruptcy?

1/20 What is Henchard's immediate plan, after being ruined?

1/21 What, in his working clothes, does the ruined Henchard wear on his head?

1/22 Where do Casterbridge's unfortunates (the *misérables* of the town, as Hardy calls them, with an allusion to Victor Hugo) like to gather, despondently?

1/23 When was the last skimmity-ride in Casterbridge?

1/24 Who looks after Henchard in his last days, and why?

1/25 What does Henchard die of?

☞ *Check answers at the back of the volume. If you scored over 15, proceed to Level Two ('Factual but Tricky'). If you scored over 10 but under 15, skim the novel again. Over 5 but under 10, reread the novel. Under 5, throw this book away and watch TV.*

Level Two: Factual but Tricky

2/1 Who is the 'Mayor of Casterbridge' referred to in Hardy's title?

2/2 What is 'almost the only attraction' of Susan's face?

2/3 Why does Henchard go to Mrs Goodenough's ill-fated furmity tent?

2/4 What two-winged creatures fly through, or around, the furmity tent?

2/5 What plague, as in Thebes under Oedipus' reign, afflicts Casterbridge under Henchard's mayoral rule?

2/6 Where, according to Solomon Longways, does Michael Henchard 'go wrong'?

2/7 Why does Farfrae stay at the Three Mariners rather than the King's Arms? And why does Susan tell her daughter they 'must' stay there?

2/8 Does Henchard break his word to Jopp, on the matter of employing him?

2/9 How much money does Henchard, with afterthought, give Elizabeth-Jane to take back to Susan?

2/10 Where does Henchard arrange to meet Susan, after he learns that she has come to Casterbridge?

2/11 Wherein, as a corn-factor, lie Farfrae's skills?

2/12 Where does Lucetta's only living relative live?

2/13 Who is characterized by 'honesty in dishonesty'?

2/14 What work task does Nance Mockridge carry out in Henchard's yard?

2/15 How long does the mayor hold office in Casterbridge, and what promotion thereafter is denied Henchard?

2/16 What dialect word in Elizabeth-Jane's mouth most vexes her 'father'?

2/17 What is 'ladies' hand'?

2/18 How many years does the judicious (and straight-talking) Elizabeth-Jane reckon her mistress, Lucetta, has before she becomes 'hopelessly plain'?

2/19 What, for those with an eye on the harvest, is the weather like in June, as Henchard's fortunes progressively fail?

2/20 Why does Henchard (in the scene of Lucetta's fainting under the pressure of having to accept his proposal) call Elizabeth-Jane a 'no'thern [northern] simpleton'?

2/21 By what right is Henchard a magistrate at petty sessions?

2/22 Who is Henchard's 'great creditor' in his time of financial distress, and why cannot Lucetta intercede with him?

2/23 How creditable, or credible, is Elizabeth-Jane's self-education?

2/24 What, according to Abel Whittle, is the advantage and what the disadvantage of being employed by Farfrae rather than Henchard?

2/25 What strange headgear (but indicative of where he has come from) does Newson have, when he comes to Casterbridge?

☞ *Answers at the back of the book. Anything over 12 is good, indicating either strong memory or recent acquaintance. Go on to Level Three ('Very Tricky—and Occasionally Deductive') which requires, in addition to intimate knowledge of the text, an ability to make plausible deductions from it.*

Level Three: Very Tricky—and
Occasionally Deductive

3/1 Is there anything to be made of the fact that Michael Henchard has never tasted furmity, while Susan has, often, as we gather?

3/2 Is Henchard's hiring Farfrae 'destiny' working its vengeful way with him, or is it to be ascribed to a defect in his chronically self-destructive 'character' (as the subtitle to the novel cues us)?

3/3 What books does Henchard prominently display in his living room?

3/4 'Casterbridge', the narrator tells us, 'announced old Rome in every street'. What can one read into this antiquarian observation, if anything?

3/5 What official post, in addition to mayor, does Henchard occupy?

3/6 Who are the principal adulterers in the novel?

3/7 Where and how does Newson 'die'?

3/8 What is the great 'national event', the occasion of the fête, which brings about the breakdown in the Henchard–Farfrae partnership?

3/9 Why does Farfrae stay in Casterbridge as a corn and hay merchant after Henchard has discharged him? Why not, as he originally intended, travel on?

3/10 Under what circumstances does Michael Henchard descend from standard English into dialect?

3/11 What does Susan ordain should be used as weights to close her eyelids, when her body is laid out for burial, and what happens to the weights?

3/12 Is Elizabeth-Jane illegitimate?

3/13 What do unruly boys do to the stone mask which embellishes the outside gate to High-Place Hall?

3/14 Hardy says that the mechanical horse drill 'created about as much sensation in the corn-market as a flying machine would create at Charing Cross'. What flying machines is he thinking of?

3/15 Why does Mrs Goodenough come to Casterbridge?

3/16 What work does Henchard accept, after his ruin?

3/17 Which psalm does the poker-wielding Henchard demand the terrified church band play for him, as they take their refreshment in the inn, and why does Henchard choose that one?

3/18 What happened to Archibald Leith?

3/19 What is the occasion of Farfrae being prematurely made mayor?

3/20 Who pays for the skimmity ride?

3/21 Who is the doctor who replaces the unfortunate Dr Chalkfield?

3/22 Who likes to see 'the trimming pulled off Christmas candles' (i.e. the high and mighty of Casterbridge brought low)?

3/23 When he treats Lucetta, prostrate after witnessing the skimmity ride, the doctor observes 'a fit in the present state of her health means mischief'. What is the present state of her health?

3/24 Where does Henchard see his 'body', and what bodies normally float there?

3/25 How many times does Newson visit Casterbridge, before being reunited with his daughter?

☞ *Answers at the back of the book. The factual questions are very difficult, and some of the questions involve interpretation. If you score anything over 10, go forward to Level Four ('The Interpretative Zone'). If your deductive answers genuinely strike you as more convincing, or ingenious, than mine, give yourself a bonus point (or more).*

Level Four: The Interpretative Zone

4/1 What, since the novel's action stops around the late 1840s, can we foresee (from historical events known to us) to be the subsequent history of the surviving characters?

4/2 Is Henchard what we (but not Hardy) would call an alcoholic?

4/3 What is Farfrae doing so far from ('far frae') home?

4/4 Hardy daringly tantalizes the reader with a huge nineteen-year hiatus, during which, we are to understand, a humble journeyman hay-trusser becomes the most important personage and dynamic businessman in Casterbridge. How does Henchard achieve this success in life?

4/5 Christopher Coney enquires, sensibly enough, why Farfrae has left his 'ain countree' if 'ye be so wownded about it'. Why indeed?

4/6 According to Buzzford the dealer, 'Casterbridge is a old hoary place o' wickedness, by all account.' What, exactly, is this legacy of 'wickedness'?

4/7 Why does Susan pass off Newson's daughter as Henchard's daughter?

4/8 Henchard tells Farfrae that he is 'something of a woman hater'. Has he contrived to keep himself 'pure' (as well as dry) during the nineteen years of his abstinence?

4/9 Why has it been Henchard's custom to 'run across to Jersey'?

4/10 What did Henchard fall ill of in Jersey?

4/11 How, as the local Jersey gossips think, has Lucetta behaved 'scandalously'?

4/12 Why does Elizabeth-Jane not recognize her mother's handwriting in the letter summoning her to a meeting with Farfrae?

4/13 Is it plausible that Lucetta (the mysterious 'lady') could be as unknown to Elizabeth-Jane as she is, given the smallness of Casterbridge? And could this rich visitor to the town have bought High-Place Hall without Henchard's knowing all about it? Or *something* about it?

4/14 Why does Lucetta choose to settle in Casterbridge?

4/15 What (despite her former prejudices) makes Lucetta amenable (almost at first sight) to the attentions of a 'tradesman' like Farfrae?

4/16 Who is 'the only one in Casterbridge' who knew that Lucetta 'came truly from Jersey' (not, as she claims, Bath)?

4/17 How, actually, has Lucetta 'compromised' herself, in her earlier relationship with Henchard?

4/18 Where could the furmity woman have, legally, committed her 'nuisance', rather than by the church?

4/19 Why is Henchard content for Elizabeth-Jane to leave his household?

4/20 Why does Lucetta go back on her pledge to marry Henchard and give herself to another?

4/21 Is it plausible that Elizabeth-Jane would not know that her mistress (and by now close friend) was getting married? When, for example, the band has been arranged to play at the reception, vast amounts of food ordered, and the church bells have been ordered to be rung?

4/22 Farfrae, we are told, 'had no suspicion whatever of any antecedents in common between her [Lucetta] and the now journeyman hay-trusser'. He does not, that is, know of the affair on Jersey. Is this likely?

4/23 Does Farfrae really not understand the hurt and injury which Henchard feels and that 'Henchard, a poor man in his employ, was not . . . the Henchard who had ruled him'?

4/24 Why, with Farfrae at his mercy after their gladiatorial combat, does Henchard not kill his opponent?

4/25 When told by Henchard that his wife and daughter are dead, why does Newson not want to see their graves, or even ask how it was they died?

☞ *Check answers at the end of the book. Give yourself a bonus for every interpretative answer which seems to you (1) correct (2) more plausible, witty, or ingenious than that which I offer.*

Total all your marks. If you scored 100 (or more), write your own book. Over 60, congratulations; 30 or less— you will have the pleasure of rereading **The Mayor of Casterbridge.**

The Woodlanders

Introductory Note on the Novel

Hardy had planned a 'woodland story' as early as 1874. He eventually wrote the work, much later in his career, for *Macmillan's Magazine*, in whose pages it was serialized, monthly, from May 1886 to April 1887, before publication in the standard three-volume 'library edition', under Macmillan's imprint. Hardy, a conscientious reviser of his work, made various textual changes in subsequent reissues of the work. But all the surviving evidence shows Hardy from the beginning in control of his intentions and materials. There were the inevitable protests against the depraved morality of the novel—particularly those sections dealing with Fitzpiers's philandering with the high and low womanhood of Hintock.

Level One: Brass Tacks

1/1 The first character we are introduced to in the narrative shows himself not to be a local in Hintock by his 'rather finical style of dress'. Who is he?

1/2 Where and how did Mrs Charmond notice that Marty's magnificent mane of hair, her only claim to beauty, 'exactly' matched her own?

1/3 What happened when a parcel of Fitzpiers's books was delivered, by mistake, to the vicarage and opened by the unsuspecting parson's wife?

1/4 How much older than Grace is Giles?

1/5 How long has Grace been away, being 'finished' on the Continent?

1/6 Of what does Grace dream, on her first night back at Hintock?

1/7 Does Hintock House stand high or low in the landscape?

1/8 What are Marty South's 'three headaches'?

1/9 Who is Giles's 'trusty man and familiar' (i.e. factotum servant)?

1/10 What, according to Mr Melbury, characterizes the distinctive Hintock gait?

1/11 How do Melbury's huge timber wagons signal to other road users that a large load is on the road?

1/12 How does Fitzpiers spend his first Midsummer Eve in Hintock?

1/13 The maidens' vigil on Midsummer Eve is broken up by a visitation of, as they think, 'Satan pursuing us with his hour-glass'. What have they in fact seen?

1/14 What, according to Tangs the elder, would cure Melbury of his obsession with his only child?

1/15 What does Fitzpiers intend doing after marriage?

1/16 How does Grace identify the faithless arm, which lets a scantily dressed Suke out of Fitzpiers's house at dawn?

1/17 What does Tim Tangs, Suke's (dangerous) fiancé, do for a living?

1/18 Why does Fitzpiers decide to put black plaster (rather than skin-coloured plaster) on Mrs Charmond's minor scratch?

1/19 What does the narrative instruct us is the 'one word' which describes Felice Charmond?

1/20 What adjective describes Suke Damson?

1/21 What is the name of the frisky horse which (when he mistakes it for torpid Darling) brings Fitzpiers to grief?

1/22 What does Melbury keep in his 'pilgrim's flask' when he undertakes journeys on horseback of twelve miles or more, and what are the fatal consequences of his flask?

1/23 What mistake in entertaining Grace in Sherton does Giles Winterborne (her suitor once more) make?

1/24 What is the name of Giles's habitation in the woods, after he loses his tenure of the cottages with South's death?

1/25 Who, alone, 'approximated to Winterborne's level of intelligent intercourse with Nature'?

☞ *Check answers at the back of the volume. If you scored over 15, proceed to Level Two ('Factual but Tricky'). If you scored over 10 but under 15, skim the novel again. Over 5 but under 10, reread the novel. Under 5, throw this book away and watch TV.*

Level Two: Factual but Tricky

2/1 To what does Percomb shrewdly attribute Marty's reluctance to part with her crowning glory?

2/2 What, when he was a child, burned a sense of his social degradation into Melbury and fired him with the ambition that *his* child, at least, should rise to a higher station in life?

2/3 Why does Marty wear pattens when walking the six miles and back to Sherton-Abbas?

2/4 Why is Giles 'not a very successful seller either of his trees or of his cider', excellent though both are?

2/5 What are the faggots, produced in such numbers in the woodland, used for?

2/6 How many candles does Grace use in preparing her toilette for her visit to Mrs Charmond, hopeful as she is that a good impression will lead to employment as the rich woman's companion?

2/7 How has Mrs Charmond come to be the 'Lady of the Manor'?

2/8 Why does Mrs Charmond want a companion on her trip to the Mediterranean?

2/9 Why does Mrs Charmond, in the event, not employ Grace who is, in every sense, eligible to be her travelling companion and amanuensis?

2/10 Why does Marty habitually call Giles (who calls her 'Marty') 'Mr Winterborne'?

2/11 What misfortunes befall Grace's 'fashionable attire . . . lately brought home with her from the Continent' at Giles's 'randy-voo'?

2/12 Under what two (different) misapprehensions does Fitzpiers labour on his first sightings of Grace?

2/13 What is the significance of John South's death, and how old is he when he dies?

2/14 What is John South's monomania and what is Fitzpiers's cure for it?

2/15 What does Mrs Charmond, through her agent, do with the cottages that come into her possession with the death of John South?

2/16 Who tells Fitzpiers who Grace *really* is (no lady, but the daughter of the local timber-merchant) and what is the high-born doctor's reaction?

2/17 Watching Marty's deftness at barking fallen timber, compared with her male co-workers, Fitzpiers notes, 'You seem to have a better instrument than they.' Is her barking-knife sharper, or finer?

2/18 What happens to the timber that we see cut and hauled off in the course of this novel?

2/19 Where does Fitzpiers want to get married, and why?

2/20 Who was Fitzpiers's landlady, before he married and took up residence with the Melburys? How does his former landlady react to his happy event?

2/21 Where, and how, does Mrs Charmond overturn her carriage?

2/22 How old is Melbury?

2/23 What, in the small part she plays in the central love triangle (Felice–Fitzpiers–Grace), is Marty South's 'one card'?

2/24 Where do Fitzpiers and Felice run away to?

2/25 Who gives Melbury the disastrously wrong information about what the new, 1857, Divorce Act will afford Grace?

☞ *Answers at the back of the book. Anything over 12 is good, indicating either strong memory or recent acquaintance. Go on to Level Three ('Very Tricky—and Occasionally Deductive') which requires, in addition to intimate knowledge of the text, an ability to make plausible deductions from it.*

Level Three: Very Tricky—and Occasionally Deductive

3/1 What do Barber Percomb, Mrs Charmond, and Dr Fitzpiers have in common?

3/2 What was the 'trick' that the young Mr Melbury played by which he won his first wife from his friend, Giles Winterborne's father?

3/3 Why did Melbury go to the trouble of having his daughter Grace 'inoculated for the small-pox', something that is still, ten years later, a wonderful event to the (un-inoculated) locals?

3/4 What does Marty hear from within Mrs Charmond's carriage, as she (Marty) is given a lift on the box back from Sherton to Hintock?

3/5 What is it, the narrator informs us, that makes 'life what it is'?

3/6 With what does Fitzpiers first look at Grace? His naked eye?

3/7 What do Mr and Mrs Melbury wear to Giles's 'randy-voo', intended to welcome Grace back as his lover?

3/8 What, as he nostalgically reminisces, do we gather was Robert Creedle's favourite public entertainment in the good old days of Wessex?

3/9 What, other than their suit and number markings, do Giles's playing cards have on them?

3/10 How does Robert mitigate the offensiveness of the slug which, unhappily, was served up with Grace's winter greens, at Giles's unlucky festive supper?

3/11 What does Giles rename the mare that he buys for Grace, and what eventually happens to the animal?

3/12 Who calls Melbury an 'old buffer' and with what effect?

3/13 Old Grammer Oliver catches a cold ('my wind-pipe is furred like a flue'). What are the momentous consequences for Grace?

3/14 What does Fitzpiers feel for the woodland region in which he has chosen to pursue his career?

3/15 How, ingeniously, does Fitzpiers explain Suke's being at his house at dawn, and how, fortuitously, does Grace later discover that the explanation is a barefaced lie?

3/16 What precipitates Fitzpiers's professional decline, after marriage?

3/17 What is the first occasion after marriage that Fitzpiers leaves home without a farewell kiss to Grace?

3/18 Why does Suke consistently mis-address Grace as 'Miss Melbury'?

3/19 What, when an exhausted Darling brings an even more exhausted (and sleeping) Fitzpiers back to Hintock (after a clandestine visit to Felice at Middleton Abbey), are the first words that he says to his anxious wife?

3/20 Giles has a 'serious illness' during the winter, before the breakdown of the Fitzpiers marriage. What was the illness?

3/21 What spurious reason does Fitzpiers give for abandoning Grace, in the parting letter he sends her?

3/22 How, in his few intimate moments with her (and harking back, presumably, to their childhood years), does Giles Winterborne address the woman he has previously called 'Mrs Fitzpiers'?

3/23 Where is Felice buried, and where is Giles buried; and who faithfully attends their graves?

3/24 What does the vengeful Tim Tangs catch in the man-trap that he lays for Fitzpiers?

3/25 What is Marty's final epitaph on Giles?

☞ *Answers at the back of the book. The factual questions are very difficult, and some of the questions involve interpretation. If you score anything over 10, go forward to Level Four ('The Interpretative Zone'). If your deductive answers genuinely strike you as more convincing, or ingenious, than mine, give yourself a bonus point (or more).*

Level Four: The Interpretative Zone

4/1 In his Preface, Hardy claims that 'the question of matrimonial divergence' (i.e. divorce) 'is left where it stood'. Although not what the Victorians called a 'social problem novel', does *The Woodlanders* hint at any Hardyan solution?

4/2 Is Marty South a waif, or what the late Victorians called 'a new woman'?

4/3 Is Mrs Charmond a good Lady of the Manor?

4/4 Why did Melbury send his daughter off to distant boarding school (where she remains, apparently, even during school holidays)?

4/5 What do we know of Mrs Charmond's late husband?

4/6 What, if anything, indicates a certain sexual laxity in the lines of Fitzpiers's features?

4/7 What are the two things we know Marty to write in the course of the novel?

4/8 Three women, as Fitzpiers watches, pass through the newly painted swing-gate by his front door. How different are their actions, and reactions?

4/9 What are the implications of Fitzpiers's affection for the poetry of Shelley?

4/10 Why will Fitzpiers not rise in the 'profession he had chosen', even if (as his saving Grace from typhoid indicates) he is a skilled medical practitioner by the standards of his time?

4/11 How does Grace find Fitzpiers when she calls on him to plead for Grammer Oliver's brain?

4/12 'Never could I deceive you,' protests Fitzpiers, 'fervently', on his first meeting with Grace. The narrator observes: 'Foreknowledge to the distance of a year or so, in either of them, might have spoilt the effect of that pretty speech.' Why does Hardy give his narrative game away in this way?

4/13 Watching Fitzpiers make his addresses to Grace, and the simultaneous accidental falling of two nesting 'love birds' (pheasants, presumably) into the bonfire beneath, what does the rural philosopher Marty say?

4/14 Mrs Charmond's discarded lover explains to Giles that he is 'an Italianized American, a South Carolinian by birth . . . I left my native country on the failure of the Southern cause, and have never returned to it since.' Is this statement something the novel otherwise generally lacks, a precise dating reference?

4/15 What do we know of Fitzpiers's background?

4/16 What do we know of Mrs Charmond's background?

4/17 What, by way of refreshment, does Mrs Charmond offer Fitzpiers when he comes to attend on her for the first time?

4/18 What reason does Fitzpiers give for taking up horse-riding (on the docile grey mare, Darling) and what is his real reason?

4/19 Does Winterborne ever do anything to or with Grace that could be thought to fall below the high standards of sexual morality he sets himself?

4/20 When the two women are lost, like babes in the wood and, despite their rivalry, huddle together for warmth, Felice whispers a few words in Grace's ear which produce a convulsive effect.

'He's had you!' exclaims Grace. 'Can it be—can it be!' What are the 'few words'?

4/21 Is there any occasion on which the three women we know Fitzpiers has slept with during the novel come together?

4/22 Who are the only patients we know Fitzpiers has cured in his medical career?

4/23 What is the only housework, so to call it, that we witness Felice Charmond performing?

4/24 When a shattered Melbury returns from London, with the news that, after all, 'unmarrying' is not simple, he explains, bitterly: 'He has not done you *enough* harm.' What does he mean?

4/25 How does the Fitzpiers–Charmond liaison end?

☞ *Check answers at the end of the book. Give yourself a bonus for every interpretative answer which seems to you (1) correct (2) more plausible, witty, or ingenious than that which I offer.*

Total all your marks. If you scored 100 (or more), write your own book. Over 60, congratulations; 30 or less— you will have the pleasure of rereading **The Woodlanders**.

Tess of the d'Urbervilles

Introductory Note on the Novel

Hardy made an agreement with the fiction syndicate, W. F. Tillotson & Son, for the novel which eventually became *Tess of the d'Urbervilles*, as early as June 1887. Prophetically, Tillotson's were appalled at the immorality of the story when they actually saw the first chapters. So too were the editors of *Murray's Magazine* and *Macmillan's Magazine*, to both of whom Hardy showed the manuscript. The novel was eventually serialized in the *Graphic* newspaper, from July 1891 to December 1891, before being issued in three volumes by Osgood, McIlvaine & Co. at the end of 1891 (it would be one of the last novels to be so published in the 'three-decker' library format). The *Graphic*, despite its name, insisted on considerable bowdlerization—involving a trick marriage imposed on Tess by Alec, the removal of her illegitimate child, and no Chaseborough orgy. It was not until 1912, in the Macmillan 'Wessex' edition, that the novelist got his narrative into the shape in which he finally wanted it. The complicated textual history of the novel, and the protests its 'frankness' provoked, are fully covered in the textual notes to the Oxford World's Classics edition.

Level One: Brass Tacks

1/1 Who informs Jack Durbeyfield about his noble pedigree?

1/2 Who, as best the reader can piece together, are the Durbey-field children and what are their ages?

1/3 Where is the d'Urberville family vault, and what does the place-name mean?

1/4 What is the name of the Durbeyfield horse and how old is he?

1/5 Is the carcass of Prince dispatched to the knacker's yard?

1/6 Where do the Stoke-d'Urbervilles live?

1/7 Where does the Stoke-d'Urberville money come from?

1/8 When we first meet him, Alec is smoking. What?

1/9 How does Alec, squire that he is, first address Tess?

1/10 Is Alec, as the reader first encounters him, bearded?

1/11 What variety of strawberry does Alec intrude, suggestively, into Tess's mouth?

1/12 What is the 'abiding defect' of Trantridge?

1/13 What does it mean when a cow goes 'azew'?

1/14 What instrument does Angel play, and where did he get it?

1/15 Which three girls does Tess share her bedchamber with and what do we know about them?

1/16 How far does the gallant Angel have to carry the girls across the flooded lane, on their way to church?

1/17 Where was Tess Durbeyfield born?

1/18 What had Tess 'hoped to be'?

1/19 What happens to the confessional letter Tess sends Angel?

1/20 Where does Angel resolve to go, after the separation?

1/21 Whom is Tess reunited with at Flintcomb–Ash, working in the fields?

1/22 How long must Tess, effectively an indentured serf, work for Farmer Groby?

1/23 Who dies first, Jack or Joan Durbeyfield?

1/24 Where does Tess 'give herself' to Alec, as opposed to being 'taken' by him, sexually?

1/25 Whom does Mercy Chant finally marry?

☞ *Check answers at the back of the volume. If you scored over 15, proceed to Level Two ('Factual but Tricky'). If you scored over 10 but under 15, skim the novel again. Over 5 but under 10, reread the novel. Under 5, throw this book away and watch TV.*

Level Two: Factual but Tricky

2/1 *Tess of the d'Urbervilles* is a novel named after its heroine. What other names is the 'pure woman' known by in the narrative?

2/2 The reader first encounters Tess in May, walking with her 'club'. She carries a 'peeled willow-wand'. What does it signify?

2/3 How old is Tess and what does her age signify?

2/4 How far is the Vale of Blackmoor from London?

2/5 When did Tess leave the village school?

2/6 What are the crest and arms of the Stoke-d'Urbervilles?

2/7 When he first meets Tess, Alec, the cad, is fascinated by one particular aspect of her physical appearance. What is it?

2/8 When Alec comes calling to see if she will accept employment with his ('their') family, where does Tess go to think it over?

2/9 What, according to Joan Durbeyfield, is Tess's 'trump card'?

2/10 What is Tess employed to do by the d'Urbervilles?

2/11 What colour are Tess's eyes?

2/12 What is 'Dairyman Dick' called on Sundays?

2/13 What is Angel's ambition in life, during his stay at Talbothays?

2/14 What gives Dairyman Crick's butter a 'twang'?

2/15 Whom was Marian, Tess's comrade, going to marry, before she fell hopelessly in love with Angel?

2/16 Whom do Angel's parents intend their son to marry?

2/17 What ominous event commemorates the marriage of Tess and Angel?

2/18 What quotation (mangled) from Browning passes through Angel's mind as he and Tess part?

2/19 Whom does Angel ask to accompany him to Brazil?

2/20 What does Marian call Flintcomb-Ash?

2/21 How does Tess celebrate her first wedding anniversary?

2/22 What happens to Tess's boots, when she makes her abortive visit to her in-laws?

2/23 What work does Tess first do in the fields, having taken responsibility for supporting her family?

2/24 What is the form of Alec's proposal to Tess?

2/25 Where do Angel and Tess finally consummate their marriage?

☞ *Answers at the back of the book. Anything over 12 is good, indicating either strong memory or recent acquaintance. Go on to Level Three ('Very Tricky—and Occasionally Deductive') which requires, in addition to intimate knowledge of the text, an ability to make plausible deductions from it.*

Level Three: Very Tricky—and Occasionally Deductive

3/1 How is Jack, Tess's father, related to the d'Urberville line if that line (originating with the Norman invaders) is, as we are told, 'extinct' and the name no longer current in the almanacs of British nobility?

3/2 Name the three Clare brothers in order of age. What are they doing when we first encounter them? Are there other Clare siblings?

3/3 Does Tess take after her mother or her father?

3/4 How does Prince die, and why does the tragedy happen?

3/5 When and how did Tess pick up her dairymaid skills?

3/6 How does Tess arrive at Trantridge to work?

3/7 Where does Mrs d'Urberville keep her bullfinches?

3/8 What is 'scroff' and what part does it play in Tess's downfall?

3/9 Who is Car Darch and what is her nickname?

3/10 How long does Tess stay at Trantridge before returning home, 'a maiden no more'?

3/11 What is the name of Tess's child, and who christens the babe?

3/12 What urn does Tess raise over her child's grave?

3/13 What are the names of Tess's favourite eight cows among the ninety-five in the Crick herd? Which is she milking when Angel 'almost' kisses her and says he loves her? How does the cow react?

3/14 What present does Mrs Crick send Mrs Clare, Angel's mother, the clergyman's wife, and what does Mrs Clare do with it?

3/15 What text was it on which the Revd Clare (Angel's father) preached (in the distant past) which so annoyed young Alec?

3/16 What happens to faithless Jack Dollop, a warning to other breakers of young girls' hearts?

3/17 Does Tess, under twenty-one, need permission to marry?

3/18 When do Tess and Angel determine to marry?

3/19 Whence arises the d'Urberville 'curse', mentioned several times in the text?

3/20 How do Retty, Izz, and Marian react to the marriage of Angel and Tess?

3/21 When, on the 'honeymoon', Angel sleepwalks into Tess's bedroom, what does he say and what does it mean?

3/22 Does Tess know that Angel has gone to Brazil?

3/23 When, persecuted by rumour and gossip from Trantridge, Tess sleeps in the wood by Chalk-Newton, whom does she have for company?

3/24 What does the 'Cross-in-Hand' commemorate?

3/25 What does Alec, after being born again a Christian, take up by way of occupation?

☞ *Answers at the back of the book. The factual questions are*
very difficult, and some of the questions involve interpret-
ation. If you score anything over 10, go forward to Level
Four ('The Interpretative Zone'). If your deductive answers
genuinely strike you as more convincing, or ingenious, than
mine, give yourself a bonus point (or more).

Level Four: The Interpretative Zone

4/1 Hardy subtitled his novel 'A Pure Woman', in oblique antithesis to such section titles as 'Maiden' and 'Maiden No More'. What would have been the resonances of 'pure' to the late Victorian ear?

4/2 What do we know of the d'Urbervilles and what, historically, does the name imply?

4/3 What is Tess's mother singing when we first encounter her and what does the song signify?

4/4 How well educated is Tess?

4/5 What is the significance of the name 'Abraham', bestowed on the sickly eldest son and heir of the Durbeyfield family?

4/6 When he is sent to Rolliver's off-licence establishment to bring back his inebriated father, Abraham overhears the drunken boast that Tess will marry a rich d'Urberville relative 'and we'll ride in her coach, and wear black clothes'. Why black?

4/7 While they are carting the beehives to Casterbridge (a journey which will end in disaster and the death of Prince), Abraham asks Tess if the stars are 'worlds'. Yes, she replies. Some are splendid and some are 'blighted'. What has put this idea into Abraham's head and what prompts Tess's answer?

4/8 What would be the contemporary resonance of the remark about Mrs d'Urberville that she 'was not the first mother to love her offspring resentfully, and to be bitterly fond'?

4/9 After Tess leaves Trantridge what does a distraught Alec do, and why?

4/10 Does Alec (who once said 'I'll never do anything against your will') 'rape' Tess?

4/11 Does Tess know for certain that she is pregnant when she and Alec part?

4/12 What may we assume about Angel's politics?

4/13 Tess is milking when Angel first declares his love, and skimming milk in the churn when he proposes. What is she doing when she says she will, soon, give him an answer to his proposal? And what is she doing when she finally says yes, she will marry him?

4/14 What is Angel's wedding-night 'confession' to Tess?

4/15 Tess tells Angel, 'you can get rid of me . . . By divorcing me'. Can he?

4/16 Tess thinks of hanging herself with the cord of a box, on her disastrous wedding night. Why does she refrain?

4/17 How much money does Angel give Tess on their parting, and what does she do with it?

4/18 What does Angel Clare, in his distress, whisper in the ear of Mercy Chant and what is her reaction?

4/19 How does Hardy describe the unnaturalness of the depopulation of the Wessex countryside and the drift of uprooted families like the Durbeyfields to towns, where destitution awaits them?

4/20 Why, as we eventually learn, did Alec never try to find out anything about Tess, after she left Trantridge? Why, for example, did he not trouble to enquire whether or not she was pregnant after their night in The Chase?

4/21 Does Tess 'murder' Alec?

4/22 How do the police know that Mr and Mrs Angel Clare are at Stonehenge?

4/23 Angel, at the time of Tess's arrest at Stonehenge, kneels alongside Tess as she lies outstretched on the sacrificial altar. Is he perhaps praying?

4/24 Is Tess pregnant at the time of her execution?

4/25 At the end of the novel, Angel it seems will want to marry his deceased wife's sister, Liza-Lu. Can he?

☞ *Check answers at the end of the book. Give yourself a bonus for every interpretative answer which seems to you (1) correct (2) more plausible, witty, or ingenious than that which I offer.*

Total all your marks. If you scored 100 (or more), write your own book. Over 60, congratulations; 30 or less—you will have the pleasure of rereading **Tess of the d'Urbervilles**.

Jude the Obscure

Introductory Note on the Novel

The novel usually taken as Hardy's (disgusted) farewell to novel-writing. Under different titles (*The Simpletons*, then *Hearts Insurgent*) the narrative was first serialized (somewhat bowdlerized) in America in *Harper's New Monthly Magazine*, December 1894–November 1895. It was published in one volume (the three-decker form now having been superseded) in 1895 under the Osgood, McIlvaine & Co. imprint. The novel provoked a storm of criticism for its alleged 'anti-marriage' doctrines. *Jude the Obscure* coincided with the breakdown of the novelist's own marriage and a flirtation with the 'New Woman' novelist, Florence Henniker—supposed to have been one of the 'originals' for Sue Bridehead.

Level One: Brass Tacks

1/1 Jude is eleven years old at the time of the novel's opening, as Phillotson takes his leave of Marygreen. The little boy has, we learn, only attended 'night school' with the village teacher. Why?

1/2 What task is Jude engaged on when we first encounter him?

1/3 What is the oldest, and what the newest, public structure in Marygreen?

1/4 What did Jude's father die of?

1/5 How long has Jude been residing with his great-aunt Drusilla, as the novel opens?

1/6 What is the picture on the wall of the inn where Jude takes Arabella on the first time they go walking, on Sunday?

1/7 Where does Arabella go, after deserting Jude, and why?

1/8 What 'idols' does Sue buy, and what does she tell Miss Fontover they are?

1/9 How does Jude raise the money to return to Marygreen?

1/10 Where would Sue rather sit than in the cathedral?

1/11 What musical instrument does Jude play?

1/12 What wedding present does Jude give Sue?

1/13 What is the 'turning-point in Jude's career'?

1/14 What is it that gives Mr Phillotson earache?

1/15 Where did Gillingham and Phillotson go to school, and where to college?

1/16 What does Gillingham suggest is the best remedy for Sue, the errant wife of his best friend?

1/17 What is Phillotson's hobby?

1/18 Who is 'Age masquerading as Juvenility'?

1/19 Why does Sue object so vehemently to the Register Office wedding which has been arranged?

1/20 What 'failing' do Jude and Sue share and is it, in fact, a defect?

1/21 How much does Arabella pay Physician Vilbert for the love philtre, and what is it (allegedly) made from?

1/22 What was the scandal at Gaymead church?

1/23 Jude's first symptoms of the sickness which will eventually kill him show themselves at Aldbrickham. What is the sickness?

1/24 What, as we learn late in the novel, was Jude's nickname among his workmates when he first came to Christminster?

1/25 What ceremony is going on, noisily, as Jude dies?

☞ *Check answers at the back of the volume. If you scored over 15, proceed to Level Two ('Factual but Tricky'). If you scored over 10 but under 15, skim the novel again. Over 5 but under 10, reread the novel. Under 5, throw this book away and watch TV.*

Level Two: Factual but Tricky

2/1 Like many novelists, Hardy tried out a number of titles before coming up with the (lugubrious) *Jude the Obscure*. Among his trial titles were 'The Simpletons', 'Hearts Insurgent', and 'The Recalcitrants'. These are all plural, while the finally chosen title is singularly focused on the named hero (who was also, at one point, less felicitously named 'Jack'). Who, other than Jude, was simple, recalcitrant, or the owner of an insurgent heart? Is anything thematic to be learned from this array of discards?

2/2 Like 'former productions', Hardy insists, '*Jude the Obscure* is simply an endeavour to give shape and coherence to a series of seemings'. The usage 'seemings' is quaint. What does he have in mind?

2/3 Aunt Drusilla's first remark to Jude (after some routine complaining) is: 'Jude my child, don't *you* ever marry. 'Tisn't for the Fawleys to take that step any more.' Why not?

2/4 In which season of the year does the narrative begin?

2/5 Arabella, we are told, has the 'rich complexion of a cochin's hen's egg'. What is a cochin?

2/6 Where do the newly wed Fawleys honeymoon?

2/7 Jude has given Arabella a framed lover's photograph of himself. What happens to it?

2/8 What occupation did Sue's (unlucky) father follow?

2/9 How old is Mr Phillotson?

2/10 What do Phillotson and Sue plan to do, when she has her 'certificate' from the teaching college?

2/11 Why is Sue's excuse that Jude is her cousin not acceptable to her mentors at the college?

2/12 What is Phillotson's 'old-fashioned . . . style of shaving'?

2/13 Why does Jude warn Phillotson that it is 'dangerous' for him to sit on the bare block of stone?

2/14 What is the name of the composer of 'The Foot of the Cross' and why, may we surmise, does Hardy introduce him?

2/15 How can the Widow Edlin, in Marygreen, 'telegraph' Jude that 'Your aunt is sinking. Come at once'?

2/16 Why does the school board at Shaston require Phillotson to resign?

2/17 On a number of occasions Jude calls Sue his 'comrade'. What are the overtones of the word?

2/18 What is Little Father Time's baptismal Christian name?

2/19 Who is the one guest Jude invites to his (abortive) wedding, and why?

2/20 What great crime and punishment lurks in the background of the Fawley–Bridehead family?

2/21 What pseudonyms for Oxford colleges are given in the novel?

2/22 Sue calls herself Mrs Fawley. Does she wear a wedding ring?

2/23 What are the names of the two siblings Father Time hangs in the closet?

2/24 What did Arabella's 'mother' (i.e. stepmother) die of in Australia?

2/25 Why does Jude take Arabella into his lodgings at Christminster?

☞ *Answers at the back of the book. Anything over 12 is good, indicating either strong memory or recent acquaintance. Go on to Level Three ('Very Tricky—and Occasionally Deductive') which requires, in addition to intimate knowledge of the text, an ability to make plausible deductions from it.*

Level Three: Very Tricky—and Occasionally Deductive

3/1 What should one read into the novel's epigraph, 'The letter killeth'?

3/2 In his Preface to the first edition, Hardy claims that *Jude the Obscure* is a novel 'addressed by a man to men and women of full age'. What is 'full age'?

3/3 When does Jude's working week as a labouring stonemason end?

3/4 What Greek dramatist is Jude fantasizing that he will get around to reading, when Arabella shouts her first 'Hoity-toity' at him? And what does 'hoity-toity' mean?

3/5 Arabella's friends assume Jude is apprenticed. Is he?

3/6 What do we know of Arabella's past?

3/7 Did Arabella deliberately loose the piglets to run all the way home, on her first attempt to seduce Jude? And was the cochin egg a ruse?

3/8 What is the 'true illumination' that Jude ignores?

3/9 What is Jude's favourite tipple?

3/10 What ideal does Jude hold before himself after the university dream fades?

3/11 Jude and Sue sleep together at the old woman's cottage, on their ill-fated day's excursion. Do they do anything more than (literally) sleep?

3/12 Whose is the second photograph in Sue's cubicle (Phillotson being the first), and whose the third, which will never be there?

3/13 Who tells the authorities at Sue's college that Jude has been dismissed from his post for drunkenness and blasphemy?

3/14 Does Arabella really think that Jude had died after she decamped to Australia?

3/15 When, at Shaston, Jude—playing the eavesdropper and voyeur, as he often does—sees Sue press a photograph against her bosom, whose photograph is it? And what part do photographs play in the action?

3/16 Why does Sue say that living as she does, in intimate connection with Phillotson, is 'adultery'?

3/17 Which contingent in Shaston supports Phillotson, as he faces expulsion from his position at the school?

3/18 When do Jude and Sue consummate their love relationship?

3/19 What does it mean when Sue is described by Jude as a 'phantasmal, bodiless creature'?

3/20 Does Arabella actually remarry in Australia? Is she, in that far-off country, Mrs Cartlett?

3/21 It has been noted that the dominant image in *Jude the Obscure* is of a hunted animal being done painfully to death. How many animal deaths are described in the novel, and who kills the beasts?

3/22 Who taught Arabella to write correct letters (as she manifestly does) when her speech is so richly ungrammatical?

3/23 Why, when everyone from looking at her knows that Sue is in the last stages of pregnancy, does Father Time not apprehend that she is with child? Why does it come as such a surprise to him? ('O God, mother, you've never a-sent for another'). He has, after all, witnessed her previous two confinements.

3/24 Why, if he calls London London (and areas within the city like Lambeth Lambeth) does Hardy not call Christminster Oxford?

3/25 Why does Phillotson return to Marygreen, of all places, if he wishes to escape the scandals which have blighted his teaching career?

☞ *Answers at the back of the book. The factual questions are very difficult, and some of the questions involve interpretation. If you score anything over 10, go forward to Level Four ('The Interpretative Zone'). If your deductive answers genuinely strike you as more convincing, or ingenious, than mine, give yourself a bonus point (or more).*

Level Four: The Interpretative Zone

4/1 In his Preface to the first edition, Hardy notes that the 'scheme' for *Jude the Obscure* was 'jotted down in 1890, from notes made in 1887'. What is the significance of these dates?

4/2 What is the 'missile' which Arabella throws at Jude, to get his attention?

4/3 Is Arabella a virgin at the start of the novel?

4/4 Why does Arabella so want to marry Jude, why *must* she have him and no other young working-class man?

4/5 Arabella is 'brighter' after her interview with Vilbert, after her first lovemaking with Jude. Why?

4/6 Why is Arabella, having so wanted to marry Jude, so quick to leave him?

4/7 Why, given the huge significance it has had in his life, has Jude apparently never been to Christminster before arriving there at the age of twenty-two?

4/8 Why is it 'not well for cousins to fall in love'?

4/9 Jude has a moment of truth, like Oedipus, at 'Fourways', the doom-laden crossroads in Christminster. Could he have taken a different route in life, or is his destiny preordained and immutable, like that of Sophocles' hero?

4/10 Jude develops his passion for Sue after apparently meeting her only twice. What attracts him so immediately and fatally?

4/11 What does Hardy mean when he writes of the pupils at 'the species of nunnery known as the Training-School' that all the faces bore 'the legend The Weaker' on them, which must be, 'while the inexorable laws of nature remain what they are'?

4/12 What do we know of the undergraduate whose picture Sue has on her wall, alongside Phillotson's?

4/13 How far advanced was Arabella's pregnancy, when she left for Australia?

4/14 Why does Aunt Drusilla tell Sue, with reference to Phillotson, 'there be certain men here and there that no woman of any niceness can stomach. I should have said he was one.' What is there about Phillotson that revolts women?

4/15 What is the name of the public house that Mr and Mrs (so-called) Cartlett take over in Lambeth, on their return from Australia? How is it different from, for example, the rustic inn at which Arabella and Jude did their courting?

4/16 What hitch obliges Arabella to marry Cartlett twice?

4/17 When Sue tells Jude that she cannot give herself to Phillotson because of 'a repugnance on my part, for a reason I cannot disclose, and what would not be admitted as one by the world in general', what does she mean?

4/18 'The letter killeth'—what letter(s), precisely?

4/19 Why does Sue jump out of the window when Phillotson blunders into her ('their') bedroom, and why does she *say* she jumps out of the window?

4/20 Why does Jude, a gifted artisan we gather, not thrive in his line of work?

4/21 What *is* Hardy's view on divorce?

4/22 'They are making it easier for poor students now', says Sue. When, precisely, is the 'now' in the novel?

4/23 What is the arc of Jude's professional life?

4/24 Why do Sue and Jude not practise contraception?

4/25 What does Esther do with her hair?

☞ *Check answers at the end of the book. Give yourself a bonus for every interpretative answer which seems to you (1) correct (2) more plausible, witty, or ingenious than that which I offer.*

Total all your marks. If you scored 100 (or more), write your own book. Over 60, congratulations; 30 or less—you will have the pleasure of rereading **Jude the Obscure.**

THE ANSWERS

Far from the Madding Crowd

Level One

1/1 *With what description does the novel begin?* Farmer Oak's smile—a face-cracking expression which, as the novel says, extends the 'corners of his mouth . . . till they were within an unimportant distance of his ears'. For much of the novel, poor Gabriel will have little to smile about. Readers may note that this 'yokel' aspect diminishes during the course of the narrative as he ascends to the level of the most powerful farmer in the region.

1/2 *What are the (ominous) colours which strike the watching Gabriel's eye, when he first observes Bathsheba, perched on all her worldly goods, trundling up Norcombe Hill?* Red and black, *rouge et noir—faites vos jeux*. She has a 'crimson jacket' and 'dark hair'.

1/3 *What is the name of the cow who is the occasion of Oak's second meeting with Bathsheba?* Daisy. She is calving at the beginning of the narrative and Bathsheba's aunt keeps her for milk. A favourite (if troublesome) beast, Daisy is mentioned later in the narrative. Dogs, after they have proved their worth, like Oak's George (who also returns later) are named, as are the horses at Upper Farm, but never sheep. There is a hierarchy of farm animals, as of farming folk, in Wessex.

1/4 *Like 'Mary' in the nursery rhyme, Bathsheba, it seems (thanks to Gabriel), will have 'a little [nameless] lamb' to follow her, 'wherever she goes'. Does this lamb (like George the dog, Daisy the cow, and Poppet the mare) have any afterlife in the narrative?* No. Presumably it is promptly served up as chops for supper at the farmhouse table. Bathsheba's aunt, we deduce, is not a sentimental woman.

1/5 *What is Gabriel's first feeling, and what his first exclamation, on* *losing the whole of his flock?* 'His first feeling . . . was one of pity for the untimely fate of these gentle ewes and their unborn lambs.' His first, and only, exclamation is 'Thank God I am not married.' Typically, he does not feel sorry for himself.

1/6 *What are Gabriel's first words to Bathsheba, after his offer of marriage is declined?* 'Do you happen to want a shepherd, ma'am?' Since, at the peril of his life, he has almost singlehandedly saved her hayrick, and the barn alongside with all her crops, the question indicates unusual *sang froid*. The ambiguity (do you want someone to look after your flocks/do you want someone to look after you?) is meaningful, perhaps. If any maiden needed a guide through her emotional, professional, and financial entanglements it is Bathsheba Everdene.

1/7 *Why is 'Henery' Fray so called, and not 'Henry'?* Because 'Henery' is how he always signs his name. He insists (wrongly, surely) that it was so spelled at his christening. Orthography is, he maintains, his servant not his master.

1/8 *What is Joseph Poorgrass's great 'defect'?* Shyness. An inherited handicap. 'Blushes', he explains, 'hev been in the family for generations.' Poorgrass is one of the more lovable of Hardy's village idiots (along with Abel Whittle and Christian Cantle).

1/9 *For whom did Bathsheba originally intend the valentine which eventually (with the fatal seal 'Marry Me') is sent to Boldwood?* Little Teddy Coggan—a favourite of Bathsheba's, apparently.

1/10 *What is the 'instrument of salvation' with which Gabriel saves forty-nine of Bathsheba's bloated flock?* 'A small tube or trochar, with a lance passing down the inside.' It is not clear whether Gabriel has picked up this useful pastoral skill from his reading of the veterinary manuals on his shelf, or whether it was passed down, as shepherd lore, by his father.

1/11 *What, according to the maltster, Smallbury, is the true test of* being 'an old man worth naming'? To be as toothless as a new-born babe. His gums are a badge of pride.

1/12 *What is Troy's motto, in his treatment of women?* 'Treat them fairly and you are a lost man.'

1/13 *What are the names of Bathsheba's three female attendants?* Maryann, Liddy, and Temperance. Only the pert Liddy (Lydia Smallbury), who is more of a companion than a maidservant (as her mistress says), leaves much mark on the narrative. Temperance's name bears witness to Jan Coggan's complaint that evangelical teetotalism is making terrible inroads on rural England's traditional drinking habits.

1/14 *Which are the two horses used for the Troy–Everdene gig; and which of the married couple prefers which?* Dainty is Bathsheba's chosen animal, Poppet (with overtones of 'little darling') is Troy's favoured beast.

1/15 *What is Troy's signal to Bathsheba that he has secretly arrived at the farm?* A 'double note' whistle, 'in a soft fluty tone'. It seems to tell us something about his seductive arts.

1/16 *What is the chalk inscription on the lid of Fanny's coffin? How does Gabriel change it? And why?* Originally it reads 'Fanny Robin and child'. Gabriel crosses out the 'and child', hoping (vainly as it transpires) to save Bathsheba's feelings. Erasure has, alas, been the theme of Fanny's short existence.

1/17 *What is Bathsheba's initial reaction to what she discovers in Fanny's coffin, when she breaks it open?* 'I hate them.' Then she kneels and prays for the victims of her husband, inspired by Gabriel's pious example.

1/18 *What is Bathsheba's immediate reaction when her husband kisses Fanny in her coffin?* 'Kiss me too, Frank—kiss me.' He refuses. The emotional contradictions here are tactfully not elaborated by Hardy, but we may guess at them. It is not, presumably, Troy's principal aim to hurt Bathsheba; he is consumed by guilt: not, one gathers, a state he is familiar with, having left a trail of broken hearts (and, quite likely, lives) behind him. But he is, we may think, a rogue not a villain; a heartbreaker but not a sadist.

1/19 *How is Troy saved from drowning?* A cutter, making for a transatlantic vessel, plucks him (lucky as ever) from the waves. He promptly enlists on board as a seaman.

1/20 *What profession does Troy go in for in the United States?* He tries out as a professor of gymnastics, sword exercise, fencing, and pugilism. A few months gives him a 'distaste for this kind of life'.

1/21 *What profession does Troy go in for on his return to England?* He becomes a circus performer, playing in the equestrian melodrama of Dick Turpin and Black Bess.

1/22 *Who sees through Troy's Turpin disguise at the funfair?* Pennyways, the dismissed bailiff. It would be interesting to know what this unlikeable fellow has been doing over the years, other than vainly trying to ingratiate himself with his former employer.

1/23 *What is Joseph Poorgrass's 'old complaint'?* A 'multiplying eye'—when he drinks, he sees double.

1/24 *How long is Troy away, presumed drowned?* Just under fifteen months.

1/25 *What is Boldwood's response, on being foiled in his attempt to kill himself?* 'There is another way for me to die,' he says. He turns himself into Casterbridge jail, expecting to be hanged by the neck, and perhaps hoping to be hanged. Unlucky in everything, he fails in this aim. He will walk the prison exercise yard for the rest of his natural life. Will Bathsheba, one wonders, visit him in prison? Or send him items of comfort?

Level Two

2/1 *Gabriel first meets Bathsheba on the toll-road, as she is moving all her worldly goods to her aunt's cottage, near Norcombe Hill. He pays the toll which she has disputed, regarding it as excessively expensive. Before the encounter with the gatekeeper, out of his sight (but seen by Gabriel), the young woman admires herself in a 'small swing looking-glass'. After she has passed by, the two men agree she is a 'handsome maid' but concur that she has a great fault. What is it?* In fact, they disagree on the nature of the fault. The gatekeeper sees her besetting fault as 'Beating people down'. For Gabriel (who has seen the business with the mirror) it is 'Vanity'. Both men's analysis is prophetic. Vanity is one of Bathsheba's besetting problems. But, as the gatekeeper perceives, she is also very sharp—as her holding her own in Casterbridge's corn exchange will bear out.

2/2 *What is the occasion of Oak's second personal encounter with Bathsheba?* He brings back the hat she has lost on her ride to the Mill. She is the ever-watched, but unconscious of being watched, woman (like her biblical predecessor). The ever-watching Oak is fascinated to see her lithely leaning back as her horse passes under the low-hanging boughs. It is the equivalent of David's seeing Bathsheba bathe.

2/3 *Why does Oak dread 'the eighth day'?* That is when Daisy will run dry for the year, and Bathsheba will no longer come by his hundred-acre farm to milk the beast.

2/4 *What, as the narrative jestingly puts it, does Oak's hair look like as he makes himself presentable to bring a lamb and (thereafter) offer marriage to Bathsheba?* Among a cascade of comic similes, his poll looked like 'wet seaweed round a boulder after the ebb'. Not propitious.

2/5 *The narrative informs us that 'Farmer Oak had one-and-a-half Christian characteristics too many to succeed with Bathsheba'. What* *are these 'characteristics'?* 'His humility, and a superfluous moiety of honesty.' Troy, by contrast, succeeds with her because his philosophy is to be 'moderately truthful towards men, but to women [he] lied like a Cretan'.

2/6 *The high point in Gabriel's career is his final union with the heiress, and his one-and-only love, Bathsheba. What is the lowest point in his career?* Playing the flute, for pennies, at the hiring fair at Casterbridge. Street busking though it be, it is not unprofitable. In half an hour he earns, from the idly thrown pennies of passers-by, 'what was a small fortune to a destitute man'. The access of wealth inspires him to go to Weatherbury (giving a shilling of his 'fortune' to Fanny on the way), where the folk, rumour has it, are as 'merry, thriving, wicked a set as any in the whole county'. They will, that is, like music to accompany their merriment and wickedness.

2/7 *What is the great communal beer mug at Warren's Malthouse called, and why?* 'God-forgive-me' because, when its vast contents are drained, the drinker feels (momentarily) ashamed of his over-indulgence.

2/8 *Who is the fattest and who the thinnest among the company at Warren's Malthouse?* Jan Coggan and Joseph Poorgrass respectively.

2/9 *What are the two novels we know Oak has read?* Alongside the practical books on his shelves dealing with sheep ailments and veterinary care are *The Pilgrim's Progress* and *Robinson Crusoe* (appropriate for a man as solitary by nature as Oak, when we first encounter him).

2/10 *How did Cain Ball come by his sinister (un-)Christian name?* His poor mother, 'not being a Scripture-read woman', mistook Cain for the virtuous murdered brother, Abel. The name, once in the register, cannot be undone. But his tactful workmates call him 'Cainy'.

2/11 *What characteristic 'pre-eminently' marks Farmer Boldwood?* 'Dignity'. Until, that is, the contents of his secret wardrobe are discovered.

2/12 *How does Liddy suggest that Bathsheba find out if she will ever marry, and what is the result?* Liddy, a country girl versed in Wessex folklore, suggests that her mistress use 'the Bible and key'. A key is placed on the relevant verse in the Book of Ruth, the Bible turned, the verse read out, and a vision of the future husband is vouchsafed (as it is to Madeleine, in Keats's 'The Eve of St Agnes'). Liddy, ever sensible, comes up with the picture of Boldwood (a good master for a young woman like herself, as she may think).

2/13 *What is the name of Boldwood's farm?* Little Weatherbury Farm, also the 'Lower Farm', to distinguish it from Bathsheba's Upper Farm. He apparently owns his property (or has a lifehold lease); she is a tenant, with a more precarious hold on her farm.

2/14 *How long does it take Oak to shear a sheep?* Less than half an hour—phenomenally fast by the standards of the day. With electric cutters, champion Australian sheep-shearers can today do it in a few minutes.

2/15 *Who is the first person ever to kiss Bathsheba, and how old is she at the time?* Sergeant Troy. Twenty-one.

2/16 *Who, or what kind of person, glides through the night as silently as a woman can?* 'A gipsy man'. Building on this piece of country lore, Oak and Maryann assume that the person stealing away in the farm gig, with the horse Dainty, is a thieving traveller. It is, of course, Bathsheba sneaking away, like a thief in the night, to meet Troy in Bath—a trip whose length (and consequences) she sadly miscalculates. Would she, one wonders, go to these extremes merely, as she protests, to break the engagement? Surely not.

2/17 *What happy misfortune allowed Joseph Poorgrass to read* The

Pilgrim's Progress? *'A bad leg'—he read Bunyan's book to while away his convalescence. It is, apparently, the only book he has ever read. Oak, with his half a dozen volumes, is regarded as a prodigy of reading by the company at the maltster's. He reads even when he is not laid up.*

2/18 *What is an 'Early Ball'?* A variety of apple developed by Cain Ball's grandfather. The name evidently means that it ripens early—phasing the apple crop to last as long as possible through summer and autumn was a West Country art.

2/19 *What tipple does Troy prefer to the local ale and mead, and with what does he fuddle the farmworkers at the Harvest Supper?* Brandy—alien tipple. The strong drink is potentially disastrous in that it renders the intoxicated men incapable of helping Oak cover the gathered crops to save them from the coming storm.

2/20 *What are the only examples we are given of Troy's 'romanticism'?* His having kept a lock of Fanny's hair, his kissing her corpse in her coffin, and his erecting a fine gravestone for her.

2/21 *What (insofar as the reader is informed) is signally missing on the inscription which Troy ordains for Fanny's gravestone, 'Erected by Francis Troy in Beloved Memory of Fanny Robin'?* It does not indicate that a baby lies in the coffin with her, mentioning only her.

2/22 *What change of events brings Gabriel to be bailiff, or steward, of both the Upper and Lower Weatherbury farms?* Bathsheba's 'widowed' apathy; the onset of Boldwood's lunacy. 'Gabriel's malignant star' sets as Boldwood's rises.

2/23 *What is written in the note which Pennyways slips Bathsheba at the fair, and which Troy ingeniously steals before she can read it?* 'Your husband is here. I've seen him. Who's the fool now?'

2/24 *What reason does Bathsheba give Gabriel for finally accepting* *the marriage proposal of Boldwood?* 'I believe that if I don't give my word he'll go out of his mind.'

2/25 *How old is Troy when he dies?* Twenty-six. The fact that he is so young makes one suddenly rather sorry for him.

Level Three

3/1 *Bathsheba saves Gabriel's life, in his hut, as it fills up with poisonous carbon monoxide. Why does she venture into his dwelling place, closed as the doors and the two small windows are?* She says that when she was milking Daisy (in her nearby pasture) she heard a dog howling. She then saw George scratching at the hut door; the animal then 'saw me, and jumped over to me, and laid hold of my skirt'. One has to suspect that Bathsheba was, in addition, curious, and wanted an opportunity to investigate this handsome young man, so clearly taken with her.

3/2 *Why, after her aunt (perhaps with Bathsheba's acquiescence) has sent the wooer Gabriel away (with the falsehood that her niece has other, more eligible suitors), does the young lady chase after him?* She says that it is in the interest of truth ('I haven't a sweetheart at all'). And then she rejects him. It seems of a piece with her chronic, and entrancing duplicity—such as sending Boldwood a valentine ('Marry Me') only to follow up with the chilling declaration that she won't. Bathsheba incarnates the dilemma of nineteenth-century woman. She wants to love, and be loved, but, as she explains to an incomprehending Gabriel, 'I *hate* to be thought men's property.' She is not, we are later told, 'deliberately a trifler with the affections of men', but—whether deliberately or not—she does huge damage. Why, for example, when intending to discourage Boldwood does she concede 'Yes, I suppose you *may* think of me' but inform him that he may not think of marrying her? No wonder the man goes mad.

3/3 *Hardy includes 'The Mistake' as part of the title for the chapter*

(4) in which Gabriel makes his marriage offer to Bathsheba. Are we to take the title as meaning 'It is a mistake on Gabriel's part to think of marrying such a "vain" woman'? Or, 'Bathsheba is at pains to correct the mistaken impression given by her aunt that she has a troop of other lovers'? Or, 'Bathsheba's biggest mistake in life is not to marry the man who so faithfully loves her when he first asks'? 'All three' is the easy answer—although Gabriel's life might, for a few years (if not in the very long run) have been easier had he never caught sight, that fateful day, of Miss Everdene on the wagon. The best bet is that it is Gabriel's mistake which is alluded to.

3/4 *How does Gabriel meet Fanny Robin, and how does he discover the story of her love entanglement?* He meets her as a vagrant, on his way to Warren's Malthouse. She implores him not to 'say anything in the parish about having seen me here', not wanting to be put in the workhouse, or suspected of being a camp-following prostitute, or sent back to be dismissed from her position as a housemaid in Bathsheba's house. Good Samaritan that he is, Gabriel gives her a shilling. At the maltster's, he learns that she was Miss Everdene's youngest servant and that she has a soldier sweetheart. Still later, he learns from fellow workers at Weatherbury that Fanny was adopted and educated at the local school by Boldwood (an odd detail) who prevailed on Bathsheba's uncle to take her into service. She was clearly well educated by the standards of her class, as the letter she sends to Gabriel, returning the shilling he gave her, witnesses: '[Troy] would, I know, object to my having received anything except as a loan, being a man of great respectability and high honour—indeed, a nobleman by blood.' This is not the phraseology (vocabulary or punctuation) of an illiterate peasant girl.

3/5 *Does anyone realize that the valentine sent to Boldwood has the dangerous motto, 'Marry Me', engraved on its sealing wax?* Bathsheba apparently does not recognize the inscription. Liddy (who approves of any prospective match with Boldwood) does.

3/6 *Who, might one plausibly suggest, is the first dyslexic to be* *described in English fiction?* Matthew Moon, who can never work out whether letters like 'J' and 'E' 'face backward or forward' and, although he is literate, habitually reverses them.

3/7 *What fateful error does Fanny Robin make about the barracks-town church in which she is to be married?* She confuses All Saints' with All Souls'. It seems odd, since the banns would have had to be proclaimed there and surely, even if she were not there to hear them, it is a detail that would have been etched in her memory. Surely, too, she would have wanted to inspect the church which would be so important to her future existence.

3/8 *What ballad does Bathsheba sing at the shearing-supper, and why is it 'remembered for many months, and even years'?* 'The Banks of Allan Water'. It is memorable because of its prophetic tale of a soldier, with a 'winning tongue', winning his bride— Troy and Bathsheba's story, as will be. A number of the characters have premonitory powers: Bathsheba, for example, 'knows' that Troy will return from the dead. Troy experiences 'an awful shudder' as he prepares for his last appearance at the Christmas feast.

3/9 *What love token does Troy, impulsively, give to Bathsheba when he scarcely knows her?* A gold watch, a relic from the Earl of Severn, his father, with the Latin motto 'Love yields to circumstance'—not, one presumes, the actual motto of the family (as Troy suggests to Bathsheba) but an apology for not making Troy's mother an honest woman: the 'circumstance' of being an earl will not permit his marrying a French nobody with a bastard in tow. But an elegant apology is in order. The watch, Troy says, was given to his mother's husband, the medical man (whose services, as the Earl's placeman, were evidently paid for). One may suppose that Troy's courtship of Fanny was not accompanied by such gifts (although it later emerges he has another watch with a lock of Fanny's hair enclosed in its case).

3/10 *Troy's display of swordsmanship to Bathsheba is almost too* *obviously phallic. With what examples of virtuosity does he crown his display?* He shears off a curl of her hair with a downward cut; he picks a caterpillar off her bosom with a pointed thrust.

3/11 *Troy tells Bathsheba (falsely, as Oak easily discovers) that he attends church at Weatherbury secretly, entering by the back tower door, and remaining during the service unseen. Why would he do this, and how, plausibly, could he explain to Bathsheba (infatuated as she is) his motive for doing so?* Presumably he claims he does not, in his military finery ('brass and scarlet'), want to make any commotion among the congregation. How many of that congregation would he know? With whom, one wonders, does he stay when he comes to Weatherbury?

3/12 *To what does Bathsheba attribute her lack of 'capacity for love'?* 'An unprotected childhood in a cold world has beaten gentleness out of me.' If it has frozen her capacity for tenderness, that unprotected childhood would seem to have also rendered her unusually independent in spirit. Bathsheba says very little about her childhood. One assumes she was brought up during her father's religious-maniac, rather than erotomaniac, phase of life—possibly the grossly inappropriate name was given her, like 'Magdalen' in the nineteenth century, to remind a little girl of her sinful gender heritage.

3/13 *Instead of returning to his 'distant barracks', as Boldwood hopes, Troy (in the period immediately before his marriage) goes to Bath, 'to visit some acquaintance'. Is there anything to be known about what he does in Bath, in these tense few days?* There may be another lady in the case. He cajoles Bathsheba into marrying him by telling her that he has seen someone yet more beautiful than she in the city. She asserts to Gabriel, after the event, that she went to Bath 'in the full intention of breaking off my engagement to Mr Troy'. The threat about the other woman forced her hand (there was indeed such a rival, she insists—it was not, although the reader may suspect it was, another example of Troy's inveterate 'trickery'; cynical readers will also note that Bathsheba—

when Oak first came courting her—was not above some similar tricks of love, her aunt telling him about all the other suitors in pursuit of her).

3/14 *Who is the parson at Weatherbury, and what do we know of him?* The Revd Thirdly. He is evidently Low Church and, as Matthew Moon says, poor—he can't afford even a tin ring to decorate his clerical fingers. Thirdly is not like the new style of parsons who wear moustaches and long beards. He is generous, however. Jan Coggan recalls that when all his potatoes were frosted, the parson 'gave me a sack for seed, though he hardly had one for his own use, and no money to buy 'em'.

3/15 *What reason does Troy give Boldwood for leaving the army?* He has decided that fighting is 'a barbarous way of settling a quarrel'. And, of course, with Bathsheba's help he can buy himself out. He may perhaps fear the prospect of the overseas posting which will soon be coming. The regiment has been mustered from near Weatherbury to a distant barracks at short notice.

3/16 *What happens to the dog, a canine Good Samaritan, which brings Fanny to the Workhouse?* The hard-hearted custodians of the place stone the beast away.

3/17 *How does Fanny's corpse end up in an inn?* Joseph Poorgrass, entrusted with bringing it by cart to the Weatherbury churchyard, stops at the Buck's Head to refresh himself, meets his comrades Jan Coggan and Mark Clark, gets 'drinky', and is too late to bring Fanny for burial that day. Unhappily, Joseph's boozing results in Bathsheba finding out the awful truth about the second body in the coffin.

3/18 *After her terrible, and final, quarrel with Troy, Bathsheba locks herself in an attic. She asks Liddy to bring her books. What, particularly?* Typically, she changes her mind. First she asks for sombre works such as Beaumont and Fletcher's *Maid's Tragedy* (and Liddy helpfully suggests 'the story of the black man who murdered his wife Desdemona'). Then she demands cheerful volumes such as *Love in a Village*. Even *in extremis* Bathsheba cannot decide one way or the other.

3/19 *What misadventure befalls Fanny's grave—unlucky in death as she is in life?* A 'gurgoyle', or effigy water-spout, gushes water down on her newly dug grave, scattering the flowers, boiling the earth 'like chocolate'. The very elements, it seems, reject the Sergeant's (false?) contrition.

3/20 *Susan Tall, the termagant wife, notes that the former shepherd's garb has changed with his promotion to bailiff status. How, exactly?* 'Mr Oak' (no longer 'Gable') wears shiny boots which have no hobnails, he wears a tall hat on Sundays, and he 'hardly knows the name of smockfrock' (the shepherd's traditional full-body apron).

3/21 *Chapter 50 opens: 'Greenhill was the Nijnii Novgorod of South Wessex'. Is this a helpful comparison?* Few readers would say that it helps them to picture the rural England village Hardy has in mind. Yet lovers of fiction could not wish that, in such a narrative situation, he had come up with some such sentence as: 'Greenhill was the Lerwick of South Wessex'. Hardy surely introduces jawbreakers, and breath-takers of this kind as his version of Brecht's 'alienation effect'—a way of jolting the reader out of any easy (or sentimental) relationship with the text.

3/22 *Who is it that prevents Boldwood from turning the second barrel of his shotgun on himself?* His servant, Samway. Boldwood's suicide attempt, involving a handkerchief and his toe, seems singularly, if typically, inept.

3/23 *What is the nature of the mortal wound that Troy receives?* He is shot in the chest (through his faithless heart, presumably) at point-blank range. So close, indeed, that 'the charge of shot did not spread in the least, but passed like a bullet into his body'. This means that when Bathsheba, as part of her 'wife's duty', lays out his body, it is not visibly disfigured.

3/24 *What is Gabriel's first plan, after the murder of Troy?* He intends to go to California, he tells Bathsheba. Presumably he has been enthused by tales of the 1849 Gold Rush. This nicest of gold-diggers will, however, strike it rich another way.

3/25 *What is Gabriel's second plan?* To take on Little Weatherbury Farm. It is never clear during the novel whether Boldwood owns or rents his farm. If the former, Gabriel will be managing it for Boldwood while he is residing at Her Majesty's pleasure. After his marriage to Bathsheba Gabriel takes on the management of both farms.

Level Four

4/1 *Why 'Wessex'?* The title of *Far from the Madding Crowd* alludes (ironically) to the condescending (and sentimentally metropolitan) praise of rural life in Gray's 'Elegy in a Country Churchyard' ('Far from the madding crowd's ignoble strife | Their sober wishes never learn'd to stray'). In his Preface to the novel, Hardy explains why he chose the antique term 'Wessex' for his regional (or, as he called it, 'territorial') setting—rather than, say, 'Dorset', or the 'West Country'. It was, he said, the 'continuity' of the place and Wessex's anachronistic 'preservation of legend, folk-lore, close inter-social relations, and eccentric individualities'. Wessex, seen in this light, is a version of Wells's time machine, but travelling into the past, not the future ('The citizen's *Then*', Hardy declares, 'is the rustic's *Now*'). Put another way, Wessex is a living historical novel.

4/2 *Does Farmer Oak have a grandfather clock?* Yes, his watch ('a small silver clock') belonged to his father, and to his father's father before him. It is an unreliable timepiece, with the habit of 'going either too fast or not at all'). By night, Oak more reliably tells the time by the stars.

4/3 *What do we know of Farmer Oak's family and background?*

His father and grandfather were both Gabriels (known to the maltster, old Smallbury, and his only slightly less old son). The Oaks have been shepherds for three generations, but our Gabriel is the first to have risen (albeit with vicissitudes) to the rank of bailiff and farmer. He is literate, which his predecessors may not have been. And he is ambitious—a rising man, as Victorians put it.

4/4 *There are often overtones in the characters' names in* Far from the Madding Crowd *('Oak' is English, of ancient stock, and the strongest of trees, for example). What are the overtones of 'Bathsheba'?* All the characters fall in love with her at first sight, as does David with the biblical woman of that name (on whom he does a Peeping Tom, when she bathes). Proposals follow, precipitately. Oak loves her desperately before he knows her name (which he only finds out, after their second encounter, 'by making enquiries'). Boldwood proposes, on the strength of having seen her, from a distance, at church and in the Corn Exchange, and after the receipt of a catastrophically ill-judged valentine. Having met her just once, by night, Troy declares (while betrothed to another woman) that he loves her. Bathsheba needs only to be seen to be loved. At one point in the novel she calls herself a 'watched' woman. Other heroines of Hardy's (Tess, Eustacia, Elizabeth-Jane), much loved as they are, lack this sorceress-like power of *instantly* entrancing men.

4/5 *When a ride over to Tewnell Mill, for oatmeal for Daisy's calf, is necessary, Bathsheba's aunt objects 'there's no side saddle' (in the stable, she means: the women of the household have not ridden before her niece's arrival). Bathsheba replies: 'I can ride on the other [i.e. a man's saddle]: trust me.' What do we deduce from this?* Bathsheba likes wearing, if not trousers (it is too early for that), 'riding habits'—she is, we assume, a 'bloomer girl', or feminist *avant la lettre*. When making her appearance in the 'man's world' at Casterbridge Corn Exchange, or superintending her farm, she wears a 'skirt', not a billowing dress. She is wearing a new 'riding habit' at the sheep-washing, when Boldwood makes his first proposal of marriage. Significantly, it is when she is wearing a voluminous, all buttons-and-bows frock that she becomes entangled with Troy and his dangerous spurs.

4/6 *Why does Bathsheba's aunt lie to Gabriel, about her niece's 'many lovers'?* Perhaps to pique his interest (if so, she succeeds only in discouraging the young man). Alternatively the older (and frailer) woman may not want to lose the companionship of her niece, or her usefulness around the household. Mrs Hurst could never, for example, ride (on a man's saddle) to the Mill, to get oatmeal, or even—one suspects—tramp across fields with bucket and pail to milk Daisy. The aunt disappears from the later novel, although we may guess that it is she who takes care of Gabriel's faithful sheepdog George for a few months, while he is settling in at Weatherbury.

4/7 *What do we know of Bathsheba's background, how she came to be so named, how orphaned, and how she came to be, if not rich, prosperous?* She came into her fortune, as is common in Hardy's fiction (e.g. Damon Wildeve's sudden legacy of £11,000), by the death of a remote uncle, tenant of a fine property, Upper Farm, at Weatherbury. Her father, as Jan Coggan recalls, was 'Levi' Everdene, a gentleman tailor 'worth scores of pounds'. (Bathsheba's marriage announcement states, less flamboyantly, that she is the 'only surviving daughter of the late Mr John Everdene, of Casterbridge'.) He became 'a celebrated bankrupt two or three times', Jan says. Levi had a wandering eye—which, finally, he cured by the ingenious device of making his wife take off her wedding ring, so he could fantasize she was his mistress. Thus he could go on 'committing the seventh' (adultery) innocently. This tendency towards breaking the seventh commandment perhaps explains Levi's naming of his only child after the most glamorous (and innocent) adulteress in the Bible, the wife of Uriah the Hittite. In his later years Levi became a religious maniac (as does Alec d'Urberville, not uncommon with reformed lechers).

4/8 *What can we put together of the career and background of Frank Troy?* As we first encounter him, he is Sergeant Troy of the Eleventh Dragoon Guards, shortly to be posted away from their garrison in Casterbridge. Dragoons are mounted infantry. It is with the dragoon's broadsword—not the cavalryman's sabre— with which Troy entrances Bathsheba. On reading Fanny's letter, Boldwood describes Troy to Gabriel. Troy's mother was a French governess ('a Parisienne', as Troy grandly describes her), and he is the illegitimate son of Lord Severn. The governess's husband, whom she married before Troy was born, was a 'poor medical man'—evidently a doctor with a not very prosperous practice in not very prosperous Weatherbury. Lord Severn paid support, handsomely, to his former mistress. Young Francis was well edu- cated at Casterbridge Grammar School and, as Liddy hyperbolic- ally puts it, 'got on so far that he could take down Chinese in shorthand'. Things changed for the worse when Severn died. The money dried up. Troy tried out as a lawyer but then, on a 'wild freak', enlisted in the army.

4/9 *Why is Sergeant Troy—educated, brave, and able—no more than a non-commissioned officer?* Before 1872 commissions had to be bought. Merit was not a consideration—particularly in a crack regiment like the dragoons. Troy has hit his glass ceiling. Among other humiliations attendant on his non-commissioned rank, he must ask permission of his commanding officers before he can marry. And he is not allowed to sport a beard (as presumably, other suitors of Bathsheba do): regulations only allow a moustache. Sergeant Troy's is very fine, and he continues to sport it after his discharge from the service.

4/10 *Shepherd Oak can speak respectable 'RP' (Received Pronun- ciation)—'Queen's English'. He also, on occasion, lapses into Wessex dialect. What circumstances condition his speech?* Among his workmates, and at the maltster's, he speaks broad Dorset (e.g. 'Cainy and I haven't tined our eyes to-night'). Talking to Bath- sheba (or Boldwood), he speaks like a gentleman, not a peasant. But on the few occasions that he is angry with Bathsheba, he lapses into dialect. When, for example, as they sharpen the shears, he chides her for her levity with Boldwood, and she reminds him of his humble place in her staff, he fires back: 'if Mr Boldwood really spoke of marriage, I bain't going to tell a story and say he didn't to please you.' In return for his insolence, shears in her hand, she dismisses him—cuts him loose.

4/11 *How many animals does Gabriel kill or injure in the course of the narrative?* He shoots the young dog who worried his flock into extinction. He kills one sheep, while saving many from the deadly bloat which afflicts Bathsheba's flock, after they have grazed on young clover. He nicks the 'groin' of a sheep he is fleecing, when his own groin is nicked by the sight of Boldwood, yet again, proposing to Bathsheba. By nature he is an animal-lover, as are other of Hardy's heroes (Jude, notably).

4/12 *What is Bathsheba doing when she first meets Troy, and how does it happen?* She is making her nightly rounds, still wearing her party dress (from the shearing-supper). Her tour leads her to one of the paths to the village. In the dark, her full skirt catches on Troy's spurs—he too is in full dress, all 'brass and scarlet'. She is 'trapped' (in more than one sense), while he flirts with her, shines the lamp on her face, and pretends to cut her free. He is, he says, staying in the village (although why he should be tramping around country paths in full-dress uniform is strange).

4/13 *The cuts, parries, and thrusts of infantrymen, Troy concedes, 'are more interesting than ours', but they lack something that dragoon swordplay has. What?* 'They are not so swashing.' Swashbuckling (looking the part) is as important to Troy as doing his duty on the battlefield. It is fitting he should end playing the part of a desperado, rather than being one.

4/14 *What do the numbers 249, 8, 27, and 750 signify in* Far from the Madding Crowd? The first is the number of passes Troy makes with his sword, to impress Bathsheba. It is eight months between Oak's saving Bathsheba's crops from fire and then from rainstorm: it is also the number of years' difference in their ages. Troy has £27 in his pocket, when Fanny dies. He gives it all to the

Casterbridge stonemason to erect a fine gravestone for her. The value of the crops which Oak saves for Bathsheba Troy from the storm is £750—'in the divinest form that money can bear—that of necessary food for man and beast'. These last two should be multiplied by around fifty to give modern sterling values.

4/15 *Liddy obviously knows that Troy is a 'fast' man, and her knowing it causes a rift between her and Bathsheba. Does Liddy really not know of the affair between Fanny and Troy?* Oak knows, Boldwood knows. If Fanny writes to a stranger (Gabriel) on the subject would she, while a servant at the Upper Farm, have been able to keep her love-life entirely secret from her workmates below stairs? Clearly, from subsequent events, she has been seduced. As the marriage notice of the Troys' wedding makes clear, he was brought up locally, the 'only son of the late Edward Troy, Esq., MD, of Weatherbury'. Is it conceivable that some village eyes would not have seen, and village tongues wagged about, his paying court to, and conquering, Fanny?

4/16 *How badly, or intentionally badly, does Troy treat Fanny?* This is one of the more interestingly un-narrated parts of the novel. When his regiment is posted away, Troy evidently thinks he has left the girl behind him, as soldiers traditionally do. But this girl pertinaciously follows him to the garrison town, 'many miles north of Weatherbury'. In the barrack town, presumably three weeks later with the banns being called (Fanny being, for the nonce, a resident, like Frank), the marriage goes wrong when Fanny doesn't make it to the church on time. Troy makes it clear that marriage is no longer in prospect. People are laughing at him. Any marriage may have been invalid anyway since Fanny is only twenty years old (as her gravestone testifies) and—until she was twenty-one—would need parental or guardian's consent, to satisfy a conscientious clergyman. This is in February (the same month that Gabriel arrives at Weatherbury and meets Fanny travelling north). In July, just married, Troy—after toying with his rival—tells Boldwood: 'Fanny has long ago left me. I don't know where she is—I have searched everywhere.' Has he?

We later learn, via Joseph Poorgrass, that after living at a garrison town on the other side of Wessex, Fanny picked up a living as a seamstress 'in Melchester for several months, at the house of a very respectable widow-woman'. Too respectable, presumably, to have an unwed mother in the house. The girl was evidently expelled when her condition could no longer be disguised. When did she become pregnant? Before leaving Weatherbury? Why, after the botched marriage ceremony, did Troy (as we deduce) walk away? A quarrel? Exasperation? A misunderstanding? Cruelty on his part? Fanny makes her last fateful journey to Weatherbury on 8 October. Heavily pregnant, she intends to stay in the Casterbridge Union (workhouse). Why has she come back? To die? Does she know Troy has married? His first question to her is odd: 'I thought you were miles away, or dead!—why didn't you write to me?' He says this in a 'strangely gentle . . . voice'. He subsequently suffers an access of belated tenderness—mooning over the lock of her hair in his watch in Bathsheba's presence. Fanny, he explains, is the woman he *intended* to marry. Fanny dies in the workhouse—of complications giving birth, presumably. Her baby also dies. In the presence of their dead bodies, Frank tells Bathsheba: 'This woman is more to me, dead as she is, than ever you were, or are, or can be.' Fanny, he says, is his true wife. Does he mean this? Has he always truly loved Fanny, and been separated from her by cruel fate? Or is she another victim of his incurable trickery and falsity in love?

4/17 *Does insanity run in Boldwood's family? asks Troy (perhaps rather nervously). Does it?* Jan Coggan, the repository of Weatherbury history and lore, does recall that 'an uncle of his was queer in his head'. At the end of the novel, however, Gabriel refuses to believe that Boldwood's homicide was driven by 'insanity'—a lover himself, he knows what Bathsheba can do to a man. None the less, the quantities of women's clothes in Boldwood's wardrobe suggest an acutely unhinged mind.

4/18 *What omens, or portents, indicate to Gabriel that a terrible summer storm is on its way?* He stumbles across a large toad ('distended, like a boxing-glove') on his path, and a 'huge brown garden slug' has taken refuge on his kitchen table. The sheep in their pasture are crowded close together—nor will they move when Oak approaches them. Countryman that he is, Oak can 'read' these signs.

4/19 *Troy gives a very special watch to Bathsheba. Does he have another watch when he does so, and is there anything special about it?* After the fateful encounter with Fanny on Yalbury Hill, Bathsheba notices that in Frank's watch is a 'small coil of hair'. It is 'yellow', not raven black like Bathsheba's. It is, of course, Fanny's hair. Troy must, therefore, have had the other watch before he met Bathsheba.

4/20 *How is it that Bathsheba does not know that Fanny, one of her servants, has blond hair?* It is perplexing. Women notice this kind of thing (e.g. Mrs Charmond and poor Marty South). Troy says that Fanny has only been in the habit of wearing her tresses 'loose' recently. Liddy later says that she normally wore a cap, so the colour was not immediately visible. Bathsheba says that she only knew Fanny, 'my uncle's servant', for a couple of days. But she was in possession of Upper Farm for two months before the luckless girl set off on her journey to find Troy. And Bathsheba is very keen to find out whatever she can about Fanny and calls her a 'steady' girl—suggesting she did indeed know her personally.

4/21 *Liddy Smallbury tells Boldwood that Bathsheba has said 'she might marry again at the end of seven years from last year'. Did Bathsheba say this, and did she (assuming that Liddy is her accomplice) mean it as yet another coquettish signal to the demented Boldwood?* Liddy covers herself by saying that the remark was said 'not seriously'. Boldwood, however, takes 'seven years' very seriously indeed. He blushes when he denies to Liddy that he has consulted a lawyer. He would not have had to—the interval before a disappeared spouse was legally considered dead was well known.

4/22 *Why does Troy choose to burst into Boldwood's Christmas party, heavily cloaked?* For dramatic effect, and to play the part of a ghost returned from the dead. He has evidently picked up thespian tendencies from his starring role as Dick Turpin.

4/23 *What is discovered in the locked closet in Boldwood's house?* A large collection of women's clothes and jewellery, all labelled 'Bathsheba Boldwood' with a date six years hence. What happens to the clothes, one may wonder? If Moon is the first dyslexic to be comprehensively depicted in English fiction, William Boldwood may claim to be one of the first stalkers.

4/24 *Does Gabriel, finally, propose to Bathsheba, or she to him?* Indirectly, she does. She comes to his house. Then, cunningly, she continues by telling him that he will never know if she loves him, because he never asks. As they part, engaged lovers, she says (with some truth, but intending jest), 'Why Gabriel . . . it seems exactly as if I had come courting you—how dreadful!'

4/25 *Do Gabriel and Bathsheba have, as she demands, 'the most private, secret, plainest wedding that it is possible to have'?* No, the Warrens' company give them a spontaneous and jolly reception. It even raises a smile from the newly wed wife, who 'never laughed readily now'. A solemn union is foreseen.

The Return of the Native

Level One

1/1 *The first section of the narrative is entitled 'The Three Women'. Who are they?* Eustacia, Thomasin, and Mrs Yeobright. Hardy likes female trios—see, for example, Tess and her two companions in the Vale of Blackmoor, or Arabella and her two companions at the beginning of *Jude the Obscure*. Hardy is, presumably, playing ironically off depictions of the Three Graces, the Three Fates, etc.

1/2 *Diggory Venn has a 'van'. What draws it?* 'Two shaggy ponies'.

1/3 *Who is the man 'no woman will marry'?* Christian Cantle. The village idiot—a 'degenerate' in the terminology of the late nineteenth century. He signals that the local blood has run thin and poor over time—like the soil of Egdon.

1/4 *What, according to Grandfer Cantle, is the sole thing that can be said against mead (fermented honey drink)?* That ' 'tis rather heady, and apt to lie about a man a good while'. It gives a man worse hangovers than the 'pretty' fresh ale brewed at the Quiet Woman.

1/5 *What is Eustacia's 'great desire'?* Literally great desire—'to be loved to madness'.

1/6 *Where do Wildeve and Eustacia have their outdoor rendezvous?* Blackbarrow.

1/7 *Which of his favourite apples does Thomasin select for Clym?* Russets and ribstones.

1/8 *What play do the Egdon mummers put on for Christmas?* It is called *Saint George*. Quite naturally, Eustacia takes the part of the Turkish Knight.

1/9 *What is Clym's birth name?* Clement.

1/10 *What is the name of the inn at which much of the action takes place?* The Quiet Woman—a euphemism, presumably, for 'witch' (a role in which local gossip casts Eustacia).

1/11 *When do the peasantry have their hair cut?* Sunday morning, Timothy Fairway doing the chopping (or 'execution' as it pleases Hardy to call it).

1/12 *What dowry does Mrs Yeobright have to give Thomasin?* Her half portion of 'a little box full of spade guineas', put into Mrs Yeobright's hands by Thomasin's now dead uncle. The cash amounts to fifty for her, fifty for Clym.

1/13 *How much does Clym discover a furze-cutter earns?* 'Half-a-crown [12.5p] a hundred' faggots (later, Captain Drew says it is 'three shillings a hundred'). During the long days of summer, one of the trade tells him, 'I can live very well on the wages.' It is, presumably, only feasible in late summer or early autumn, when the crop is dry. For the rest of the year there is the option of 'turf-cutting'—peat, presumably.

1/14 *What excuse does Wildeve give his wife for his going to East Egdon, where he knows there will be a dance and, probably, Eustacia to dance with?* He tells his wife he intends to buy a horse.

1/15 *What is the signal which, in summers past, Wildeve used to announce his presence outside the house to Eustacia, so as not to arouse the suspicions of her grandfather?* He would put a moth in at the open window. It would make for the candle flame and incinerate itself—something which would attract Eustacia's attention (and, did she but know it, predict the doomed conclusion of their relationship). We are told that their affair climaxed in the late summer months.

1/16 *Which pool is dry in the heat of summer, and which still deep with drinkable water?* Bottom Pond goes dry, but Parker's Pool doesn't. Mrs Yeobright enquires of the little boy (Johnny Nunsuch) on the matter, after being excluded from her son's house. The cup of water Johnny brings her is distasteful because it is warm.

1/17 *Do Clym and Eustacia have a servant in their house at Alderworth?* Yes, a girl called Ann. Few furze-cutters can have been so provided with domestic help.

1/18 *To what does Christian Cantle liken the eye of an adder?* 'A villanous sort of black currant'.

1/19 *What, late in the action, do we learn is yet another signal that Wildeve uses to announce—furtively—that he is in the area and has come to see Eustacia?* He throws a stone in the nearby pond. The splash alerts her. Like the moth and the candle, the signal is prophetic. It will be water, not fire, that destroys them, however.

1/20 *What, as we know them, are Eustacia's last words? And what Wildeve's?* Hers are 'O how hard it is of Heaven to devise such tortures for me, who have done no harm to Heaven at all.' His are 'O my darling!' as he jumps into Shadwater Weir without even throwing off his great-coat. Is he trying to save her, or join her in watery death? The fact that the only marks on his corpse (unlike hers) are torn fingers from trying to clamber out suggests that— fickle to the end—he changed his mind once in the water and wanted to live, even if Eustacia died.

1/21 *What curse does Susan, as she destroys the effigy of Eustacia, utter?* The Lord's Prayer, backwards. The blasphemy evidently works.

1/22 *Where do Thomasin and Little Eustacia finally make their home?* At Blooms-End.

1/23 *What colour coat does the whitened Diggory appear in, when he* *introduces himself to the widowed Thomasin?* A bottle-green coat. His address is colourful—but there is no speck of red in it. Or on him. He whitened, as he tells her, 'by degrees'.

1/24 *How does Diggory indicate to Thomasin that he is presenting himself to her as a suitor?* Preserver of local myth, ancient ritual, and folklore that he is, Diggory arranges, in the jolly month of May, to have a phallic maypole (and pagan morris dancers) outside her front door, and he steals one of her gloves as a love token.

1/25 *What souvenir of Eustacia does Clym give the faithful Charley?* One of the three locks of her raven hair that he has kept.

Level Two

2/1 *What is the pace of life in the Egdon valleys?* So slow as 'nearly resembling the torpor of death'.

2/2 *Who is the native who returns?* Clearly Clym. But it could also, conceivably, be Damon Wildeve who—like Clym—gives up a promising career in the outside world to come back to his native heath. We know very little about Damon's antecedents. But why, other than that he in some way 'belonged', would he wash up in such a remote and uncongenial place?

2/3 *When and where did Grandfer Cantle enlist as a soldier?* 'In the Bang-up Locals (as we were called) in the year four'. The regiment was called 'Bang-up' for its smartness (by Egdon standards). The young Cantle was a member of a locally recruited militia, and was mustered, as he later recalls, 'because it was thoughted that Boney had landed round the point' (i.e. via the Bristol Channel). If he is now, as Timothy Fairway says, 'seventy if a day', and it is now around 1840, Cantle must have been slightly long in the tooth (not that he now has any left) even then.

2/4 *Why could the marriage between Damon and Thomasin not take* *place?* First, because Mrs Yeobright forbade the banns. Then, after she relented, 'the parson wouldn't marry us because of some trifling irregularity in the licence' (the document was made out for Budmouth, not Southerton). Third time (un)lucky. One ignores omens in Hardy's world at one's peril.

2/5 *What, to his dismay, does Captain Drew discover that his granddaughter, Eustacia, has used for her bonfire?* 'My precious thorn roots, the rarest of all firing, that I laid by on purpose for Christmas'. Eustacia likes root-and-branch destruction. More significantly, Wildeve remembers 'that last autumn at this same day of the month, and at this same place you lighted exactly such a fire as a signal for me to come and see you'. 'See' is a euphemism: the signal (one of a whole set that they have to arrange their assignations) meant she was alone, and presumably they made love.

2/6 *What is peculiar about Eustacia's eyes?* They are 'Pagan' and 'full of nocturnal mysteries'. Egdon, of course, is a pagan place and there are numerous suggestions that she is indeed a witch. 'Going to church,' we are told, 'except to be married or buried, was exceptional on Egdon.' Pity the vicar (who never appears in person).

2/7 *What is Eustacia's reply to Wildeve's suggestion that they emigrate, instantly, to Wisconsin?* 'That wants consideration.' An oddly prudent response for this impulsive woman. It may be, of course, that her geography is better than his. In the 1840s Wisconsin was an utter wilderness.

2/8 *What dream does Eustacia have, on the night of Clym's return, and how does it end?* She dreams of herself 'dancing to wondrous music, and her partner was [a] man in silver armour'. He removes his helmet to kiss her, and his body falls into fragments, 'like a pack of cards'. Prophetic, or what?

2/9 *In return for allowing her to take his part in the mummers' play,* *what does young Charley demand, and what does he get from Eustacia?* He asks for half an hour holding her hand. She beats him down to fifteen minutes.

2/10 *Who 'gives Thomasin away' at her (second) wedding to Wildeve?* Eustacia, as Venn tells Mrs Yeobright who, strangely, is not present. Venn, as Egdon's universal spy, observed the ceremony secretly.

2/11 *What is the difference between a furze-cutter and a heath-cropper?* The first is human, the second equine.

2/12 *How does Susan Nunsuch counteract Eustacia's 'bewitching' of Susan's son (as she thinks)?* The vengeful mother waits until Eustacia makes one of her rare visits to church and pricks her 'with a long stocking-needle'. Evidently a folkloric remedy.

2/13 *Which is the only season when Eustacia can bear the 'heath'?* The 'purple season', in autumn, when, like heather, the furze colours the landscape.

2/14 *Who says (as many could in Hardy's fiction) 'I am wrongly made'?* Mrs Yeobright, in conversation with Thomasin. It is not clear in what way Clym's mother is wrongly made unless she means that she is lacking in conventional maternal fondness.

2/15 *What do Christian and Wildeve use for a gaming table, and what do Wildeve and Venn use for light when the second dice game is played?* The gullible Christian and guileful Wildeve play by the light of their lantern on a 'large flat stone' on the heath. The game between Wildeve and the even more guileful Venn is illuminated—the candle having guttered out after a death's-head moth flew into it—by the light of thirteen glow-worms. The unlucky number 13 is, perhaps, a gothic touch too many.

2/16 *What, according to the Southerton surgeon, has caused Clym's eye problems?* The strain of night studies (by feeble candlelight), while suffering a cold. He is not a very impressive practitioner, one deduces, even by rural standards in the 1840s. Clym would seem to have macular degeneration, or glaucoma.

2/17 *What is it that finally prostrates Mrs Yeobright on her epic hike back from Alderworth to Blooms-End?* The bite of an adder—allusive (she having been barred entrance as she thinks by Clym) to Lear's 'how sharper than a serpent's tooth it is, to have a thankless child'.

2/18 *What medicine do the residents of Blooms-End cottages apply to the wound of Mrs Yeobright?* Fried snake. Rural homeopathy. Genuine 'snake oil'.

2/19 *What does Wildeve propose to do with his windfall?* Travel round the world, finishing up in India and then Paris. Mentioning the Paris project to Eustacia may, perhaps, be intended to rub salt into her wounds.

2/20 *Who is it that discloses that it was probably as much a broken heart as an adder sting which killed Mrs Yeobright?* Susan Nunsuch's boy, who it was gave the old lady a cup of water and was told she was distraught because she had been 'cast off by her son'. Mrs Nunsuch was the mischief-maker who stabbed Eustacia with a needle in church. Now she stabs her again, indirectly, via her son.

2/21 *Who chooses the Wildeves' baby's name, Eustacia Clementine?* It would be cruel (although not entirely out of character) for Damon to have done it (his spite sharpened by 'twankiness' at the child's sex). But it seems more likely that it is a gracious gesture by Clym's cousin.

2/22 *Thomasin follows Wildeve, as he goes mysteriously onto Egdon, on Guy Fawkes night. As he comes to a fork in the road, what does she overhear him say?* 'Damn it, I'll go!' Then, symbolically, he takes the left-hand fork rather than the right. It is strange that she can overhear him without being herself seen—but she is a country girl, light-footed, and knows the country. And of course it is dark.

2/23 *What is the name of Thomasin's nurse and what is the last thing we see her doing?* Rachel. Her last described act is hanging Wildeve's banknotes out to dry in front of the fire, like so many baby nappies.

2/24 *How many dairy cattle does Diggory's dairy have at the end of the novel?* Eighty, the same number as his father, who must, somehow, have lost his farm. Diggory's farm is at Shadwater, only two miles from Alderworth. Again it is strange that an event so close, and so interesting, should not have been common knowledge and that neither Thomasin, Clym, nor any of their servants should have known of Diggory's changed fortunes.

2/25 *What are the three activities 'alive' in the widowed and orphaned Clym?* To visit the graves of his mother and wife and prepare as 'an itinerant preacher of the eleventh commandment' —a kind of homespun Unitarianism, as it later turns out.

Level Three

3/1 *In his opening chapter, Hardy uses the terms 'heath' and 'moor' for his wild setting. What, if any, is the difference?* There seems to be no real difference, although 'moor' suggests rather more moisture in the soil. Allusions to Heathcliff (in *Wuthering Heights*) and Lear are usefully invoked by Hardy. Hardy scholars usually identify Egdon with the heath east of Hardy's birthplace, Higher Bockhampton.

3/2 *Why do farmers need 'redding' for their sheep?* The animals look so alike when grazing moor/heath, or in insecure pens at market, that it is impossible to identify who actually owns them without indelible marks (like cattle 'brands') which can be seen from a distance. Precise respect for 'ownership' of not just sheep, but marriage partners, is, of course, Diggory's higher purpose in life. Venn, a smart operator, seems to realize that the days of the reddleman are—with new efficiency (and enclosures) in pastoral farming—short. Having made his money, he gets out, marries Thomasin, and becomes a dairy farmer.

3/3 *What is the point of the 'festival pyre' which illuminates so vividly the early section of the novel?* Hardy suggests that the communal bonfires are what in the military is called a *feu de joie*—inflammatory exuberance. It is, of course, the Fifth of November and the ritual immolation in effigy of Guy Fawkes. But in the West Country, still steeped in blood from the reprisals for the Monmouth Rebellion, there is little residual gratitude for the preservation of Westminster from the rebels' explosives. The fires, Hardy tells us, link to 'Thor and Woden . . . rather the lineal descendants from jumbled Druidical rites and Saxon ceremonies than the invention of popular feeling about Gunpowder Plot'. As Christian (ominous name) says: 'I don't think fifth-of-Novembers ought to be kept up by night except in towns. It should be by day in outstep, ill-accounted places like this!'

3/4 *What is the value of the furze that the 'furze-cutters' so laboriously gather in? What is the dried weed and shrub used for?* Even by Hardy's standards, *The Return of the Native* is a novel somewhat overloaded with symbolism. The cutting of grass (albeit the coarse herbiage of Egdon) evokes the Bible (flesh is grass, cometh up as a flower, etc.), Marvell's mower, and the grim reaper with his scythe. The only temporal purpose to which we see the furze being put in the narrative is as kindling, or fast-burning fuel.

3/5 *What is indicated by the various 'braidings' of Thomasin's hair?* On ordinary working days, she braids it in threes, on Sundays in fours, on festival days in fives. And, when she marries, in sevens.

3/6 *How did Clym become a jewel merchant in Paris?* As a child,

Clym was observed to be precocious and artistic ('At seven he painted the Battle of Waterloo with tiger-lily pollen and black-currant juice, in the absence of watercolours'). The details of his becoming a jewelsmith are 'not necessary to give', we are told (or not told). On the death of his father, a patron had him appren-ticed at Budmouth—then a resort of the rich, fashionable, and bejewelled. From there he moved to London and France, pre-sumably rising in his trade. In Paris, during the decade of revolu-tions (the 1840s), he evidently imbibed revolutionary notions (hence his philanthropic, and quixotic, resolution, on returning to Egdon, to educate the peasantry—whether they want it or not—according to a new quasi-political system). We may also suspect that all the squinting at gems through a magnifying glass has disastrously weakened Clym's eyes. Taken with his strange revulsion against Paris and things Parisian, we may also suspect that the failing eyesight is the organic sickness which accompanies syphilis—although that may be a speculation too far.

3/7 *What is the second 'wound' Eustacia receives on the Sunday on which she is 'pricked' for a witch?* Letting down the rope and bucket deep into her grandfather's well at Mistover, with the assistance of Clym, she burns all the skin off her hands. 'A bright red spot' appears on the smooth surface of her hand, Hardy writes, 'like a ruby on Parian marble'. It is a simile which might naturally have come to the Parisian jewelsmith's mind.

3/8 *What, when not mumming, is Charley's occupation?* He is the groom, or stable boy, who looks after the horses in Captain Drew's stable. It is not, presumably, a full-time occupation and he may, judging by later events in the novel, do it merely to be near the woman he devotedly loves.

3/9 *What is the first, ominous, gift which Clym gives Eustacia?* A barrow (burial mound) is opened up on the heath, and the ancient tomb robbed. Clym gives Eustacia a funeral urn full, as Christian quakingly recalls, of 'real skellington bones'. Miss Vye, he adds, has a 'cannibal taste' for such things. The urn, Mrs Yeobright ruefully observes, was meant as a gift for her, nearer to death as she is than Eustacia.

3/10 *Who 'might have been called the Rousseau of Egdon'?* Wildeve. Hardy is thinking of the 'restiveness', sexual adventurism, and psychological perversity confessed to in Rousseau's (scandalous) memoirs.

3/11 *Who is the first person Eustacia ever loved with all her heart?* An anonymous officer of the hussars, whom she once saw ride down the street in Budmouth. He was a 'total stranger' and they never afterwards met—but 'I loved him till I thought I should really die of love'. She has, ever since, been waiting for her hussar Prince Charming to return and carry her off. She throws some of his glamour, spuriously, on Wildeve and Yeobright, neither of whom can live up to her ideal.

3/12 *What reason does Wildeve give for Thomasin not herself walking across all the way to collect the fifty guineas Mrs Yeobright has for her?* He reminds the old lady of Thomasin's 'present state of health'—delicately alluding to her pregnancy. Later Clym says that Thomasin will be confined in September or early October. They were married shortly after Christmas. Wildeve wasted no time.

3/13 *What ominous error arises from the dice game between Venn and Wildeve?* Venn wins all the money and (not knowing Mrs Yeobright's intention to divide it) gives the hundred guineas, including the fifty destined for Clym, into Thomasin's hand. Christian (in his shame at having gambled away the money entrusted to him) says nothing about his delinquency to Mrs Yeobright. It was grotesque of her to choose the village idiot as her delivery boy.

3/14 *Where and what is the 'gypsying'?* The dance at East Egdon where a resentful Eustacia, partly to spite Clym, goes jigging. At the dance she will become dangerously involved again with

Wildeve. One of Eustacia's ambitions in going to Paris was that she might indulge extravagantly in dancing, the pastime of which she was 'desperately fond'. With whom, though, can this solitary woman ever have danced? Possibly at Budmouth, where she lived until her late teens, she was an attender at assemblies, balls, and routs. As a little girl, she may well have attended dances at which her bandmaster father presided. Egdon is, apart from church services, a society with very little music.

3/15 *Does Wildeve report Venn's firearm assault on him to the police?* He goes to one of the two constables assigned to the parish of Alderworth but, on reflection, thinks better of making a complaint (how, he must have wondered, would he explain his being where he was, lurking outside Eustacia's house?).

3/16 *What does Venn call his campaign against Wildeve?* 'The silent system'. It was the term used to describe the prison reform, introduced at this period by the Benthamite reformers of the English prison system. His choice of this name implies that his intention is not merely punitive but, somehow, to rehabilitate the errant husband.

3/17 *Who tells Eustacia about Wildeve's inheriting £11,000, and where does the fortune come from?* Her grandfather tells her. A distant uncle in Canada died, after learning that all his family were drowned at sea. Hence Captain Drew is one of the first to find out—presumably from contacts in the marine service, from scanning the naval gazette, or possibly from Charley: it is hard sometimes to work out how news travels, or does not travel, in this world.

3/18 *Why, if he knew at the time, did Wildeve not tell Eustacia he was unexpectedly rich, from his uncle's windfall, when he visited her cottage?* Possibly because Mrs Yeobright's knocking interrupted any prolonged conversation (and the possibility that Clym, sleeping on the hearth-rug, might wake). But the reason he later gives is 'I did not like to mention it when I saw, Eustacia, that your star is not high'. It seems rather weak. It may have crossed his mind that, now that he is a lover of means, he fears that she might now take him up on the offer to elope to Wisconsin, leaving Clym to his chosen future career as Egdon's most literate furze-cutter.

3/19 *Would Clym have had his nervous collapse had he not been under the 'misapprehension' that it was he, the bad son, who was responsible for his mother's death, by two months' coldness towards the old lady?* He seems to have been having a slow nervous break-down for months. The death of his mother merely tips him in a direction he was inevitably moving. If anything, it coheres the swirling discontent of his life into a single, culpable, issue ('the very focus of sorrow', Hardy calls it).

3/20 *We are told that Thomasin's arrival in Clym's room, in his extremity of self-flagellating remorse, 'came to a sufferer like fresh air into a Black Hole'. What are the implications of the term?* The Black Hole of Calcutta, in which during the Indian uprising of 1756, some 120 British prisoners were stifled to death. A trifle melodramatic, unless we are to think Clym is dying a hundred deaths. It may be that Hardy intends us to see Clym's reactions as extravagant.

3/21 *Why is Wildeve said to be 'twanky'?* Because Thomasin is delivered of a girl rather than a boy. Would he have run away with Eustacia if he had to leave a son rather than a daughter behind him?

3/22 *What is the flaw in Eustacia's wild plan to get to Budmouth, then to take a steamer across the channel, and then Paris?* She has no money—something that seems not to occur to her until she has made firm plans with Wildeve. Then, to her horror, she realizes that she can only pay for this dream by the nightmare of liaison with her future 'protector', Wildeve, as his mistress, with all the attendant risks. She comes to this realization disastrously late.

3/23 *In his first published version of the narrative, Hardy has Wildeve intend to elope with Eustacia and abandon Thomasin. In*

*his revised version, Wildeve is made to behave more nobly—merely
assisting Eustacia's flight with the intention of then returning to his
wife. Does Hardy, in the revised version, leave any ambiguity in
Wildeve's (reformed) resolution?* Yes. It is finely poised. 'To-
night,' the reader is told, 'though he meant to adhere to her
instructions to the letter . . . his heart was beating fast in the
anticipated pleasure of seeing her.' Hardy has added in revision
the fine touch that Damon is deceiving himself.

3/24 *What happens to Johnny Nunsuch after the death of Eustacia,
the witch his mother believes (to the point of killing Eustacia in
effigy) is responsible for his illness? Does he recover?* We never know.
It is one of the intriguing hanging threads in the novel.

3/25 *Is Clym a successful itinerant preacher?* The last paragraph
of the novel suggests not, but 'he was kindly received, for the
story of his life had become generally known'. People felt sorry
for him, that is. Did they also think of him as a cuckold which, at
the cost of her life, Eustacia ensured he would never be? Probably
people did think just that, so their sympathy would have been
mixed with a certain condescending scorn to which he is literally,
and figuratively, blind.

Level Four

4/1 *In his 1895 Preface, Hardy writes: 'The date at which the
following events are assumed to have occurred may be set down as
between 1840 and 1850.' Why this antedating of a narrative published in the 1870s?* It was, of course, common Victorian fictional
practice to set back the action of fictional narrative—Dickens,
Thackeray, and Eliot routinely do it. But Hardy, returning to the
decade of his own birth, was precisely reconstructing a lost world
of childhood. The sense that *this* Wessex, so vividly remembered,
no longer exists hangs over the narrative like a dark cloud.

4/2 *Why did Mrs Yeobright 'forbid the banns'?* It is, we gather, female intuition: correct intuition, as it turns out. Mrs Yeobright is not merely an anxious but (as her inspection, for example, of the work of ants on the heath shortly before her death shows) a thoughtful woman. Wildeve is older than Thomasin and, as we learn late in the novel, she has a darling scheme that her niece should marry her son. Forbidding the banns, however, would be a dramatic act in a community as small and inbred as Egdon's. Has Mrs Yeobright picked up something about Wildeve's wild ways as a young man? Was there some sexual scandal involved in his giving up what was—evidently—a promising career as an engineer? Hardy leaves a thought-provoking pool of darkness around Damon's past.

4/3 *What was Diggory's father, and how is it the son finds himself a reddleman?* Venn senior was, we learn in passing (and rather vaguely) from Mrs Yeobright, 'a dairyman somewhere here'. Diggory 'went away' into the reddle trade. We never encounter any of his relatives. Did he run away—as a rebellious and enterprising young man (the more rebellious when disdained by Mrs Yeobright as a suitor for Thomasin)? Is Diggory another returned native? Was his dairyman father ruined? Did he, obstinate as he is by nature, quarrel with his parent? Or did he merely see a commercial opportunity (he is, we gather, well off for a peddler, or itinerant seller of services—a 'prosperous man'). Possibly, too, Diggory relishes the power that the superstitious around Egdon ascribe to him—stalking round the heath as he does like a fiery demon ('You won't carry me off in your bags, will ye, master?' the terrified little boy asks him). The reddle trade, and with it the reddleman, have, Hardy tells us, largely disappeared 'since the introduction of railways'. He would have known them as a (perhaps terrified?) little boy.

4/4 *What do we know about Wildeve's professional past?* His 'inflammability' (i.e. lust for beautiful women) 'has brought me down from engineering to innkeeping'. How, one wonders, could that decline happen? Did he neglect his study, his work, seduce his employers' wives and daughters? All these seem quite plausible.

He seems, in modern parlance, to be a sex addict—something that Eustacia dimly appreciates. 'How strange it seems,' she says, 'that you could have married her or me indifferently.' Or have loved (in his Wildevian fashion) both Eustacia and Thomasin simultaneously. Damon, it seems, can no more help himself when there is a skirt in the room than the moth can prevent itself flying towards the candle. Are female servants (Thomasin's young nurse, Rachel, for example) safe from his predatory attentions? Or the barmaids at the Quiet Woman?

4/5 *What do we know of Eustacia's past, and what has brought 'a woman of this sort' to Egdon Heath?* As the narrative declares, 'Budmouth [i.e. Weymouth] was her native place, a fashionable sea-side resort'. Eustacia was the daughter of a bandmaster of a regiment quartered there. He met his wife (Eustacia's mother) during a visit with her father, later a sea captain (Eustacia's unhappy guardian grandfather in the novel). Captain Drew spent seven years, as he recalls, 'in that damned surgery of the *Triumph*, seeing men brought down to the cockpit with their legs and arms blown to Jericho'. He was then, evidently, promoted to something better than surgeon's mate although, as Mrs Yeobright caustically notes, 'They call him Captain; but anybody is captain. No doubt he has been to sea in some tub or other.' It may be a courtesy title. The family, we learn, have a tinge of nobility. Eustacia's father had their only child well educated. Eustacia, somewhat euphemistically, describes her father as a 'great musician'. On his wife's death, the bandmaster 'left off thriving, drank, and died also' (one of Hardy's terser obituaries; he was presumably dismissed the service). Eustacia was left to the care of her invalid grandfather. He left the service after having three ribs crushed (by falling timber, in battle, presumably). He evidently survives in his airy perch at Egdon on half pay.

4/6 *Why does Captain Drew oppose the lower orders going to school?* Literacy, the crusty seadog believes, 'only does harm'. Every gatepost and barn door bears witness to the harm, 'a woman can hardly pass for shame sometimes'. His navy service has evidently made him a martinet about how to keep the lower orders in line. We never learn of any school in Egdon—that proposed by Clym would seem to be needed in one sense. But a more practical academy might serve the community better.

4/7 *What, as he tells Eustacia, has so 'depressed' Clym?* 'Life'. That, the lady responds drily, 'is a cause of depression a good many have to put up with'. For herself, she finds relief from the depression of life with 'events'. Events which she typically—and malignantly—sets in motion.

4/8 *Why, after their route to the altar has been so fraught, does Thomasin finally agree to marry Wildeve? Why, on his part (having been lukewarm or fickle hitherto), does he want—precipitately—to tie the knot? Why does Mrs Yeobright, who has never approved, go along with a hugger-mugger union, 'the day after to-morrow'?* Thomasin's explanation for accepting him is that 'I am a practical woman now' (and, being over twenty-one, indeed a woman). Wildeve's low-minded motive is to 'wring the heart' of the proud Eustacia, who has just sent him a letter of dismissal. Women reject Damon at their peril. Mrs Yeobright is keen that the canard that Thomasin was jilted at the altar should be firmly put down— as marriage will succeed in doing. Love, apparently, does not come into her calculation.

4/9 *Why does Clym 'return'?* He is pulled back, we gather, by sheer magnetic force of place, so 'inwoven with the heath' is his character. You can take the boy out of Egdon but never Egdon out of the boy. 'I would rather live on these hills', he tells Eustacia, 'than anywhere else in the world.' Hardy, too, was a returned (and not entirely easily returned) native, taking up occupation of his self-designed house, Max Gate, in 1885.

4/10 *Why does Clym think he is qualified to run a day school for children and a night school for adults? Why does he give up the worthy line of work he is trained for?* Clym, hopeless optimist that he is, thinks he can easily qualify himself to run a school; he needs only to 'study a little'. As he tells his mother, 'My plan is one for instilling high knowledge into empty minds without first cramming them.' He is, that is to say, going to teach a kind of 'philosophy'. No tedious Writing, Reading, and Arithmetic at Mr Yeobright's academy. He gives up his trade because, as he tells his mother, 'I hate the flashy business.' And presumably, the flashy, self-adorning, clientele. One assumes he has been infected by radical views in Paris.

4/11 *What is Clym's (wholly misconceived) justification for marrying Eustacia, and what is hers (equally misconceived) for marrying him?* He tells his mother that Eustacia 'would make a good matron in a boarding-school' (she certainly would not). She, on her part, wants to go to Paris and has always seen Clym as her ticket out of Egdon. They have known each other three months, but Eustacia has not informed herself as to the seriousness of Clym's resolution to stay in the area as a philanthropist-schoolteacher living, presumably, on air while he improves the local population. She fondly believes she can change his mind. But, although soft about many things, Clym is stiff-necked in his resolve to teach.

4/12 *How many weddings does Mrs Yeobright* not *attend in the narrative?* Mrs Yeobright is a staunch boycotter of marriage ceremonies. She declines to attend that at Southerton, which goes wrong. By Thomasin's request, she does not attend her niece's wedding to Wildeve in his parish. And she 'declines' to attend the wedding of Clym to Eustacia.

4/13 *Why, given his abilities, does Clym descend to the humble role of furze-cutter?* Not merely the half-crowns, although as he says every little bit helps conserve the capital he has brought back from France. The manual work 'soothes' him, we are told, and brings him into 'intelligent intercourse' (as Hardy elsewhere calls it) with his native heath. It makes him one of the toiling classes (like the Indian, or African native). There is also, as his working song ('Le point du jour') suggests, something symbolic in the work.

4/14 *When Diggory discharges his gun at Wildeve, as he loiters with lustful intent around Mistover, does the reddleman intend to wound or kill Damon?* One assumes it was a warning shot—although at night accidents will happen. Diggory seems to be armed with a shotgun—something with which he could more innocently shoot birds for his table. We are told 'a few spent gunshots fell among the leaves'—pellets, not bullets, apparently. At point-blank range shotguns can be lethal in Hardy's world, as Boldwood's is.

4/15 *When Clym, the 'native', tells his wife that had he never 'returned' the destinies of three people would have been very different (meaning himself, herself, and his mother), what does Eustacia think?* 'Five . . . but she kept that in.' She is thinking, of course, of Mr and Mrs Wildeve.

4/16 *Does Wildeve intend seduction when he visits Eustacia by night and by day?* It may be that he simply wants to assert his old charm over a former conquest. But Eustacia assumes it is her body he lustfully and adulterously wants and tells him that she 'spurns' the offer of his renewed love.

4/17 *Is it likely that Mrs Yeobright, although she has never been to her son's house at Alderworth, would not know (even roughly) where it was located (about five miles away; easy walking distance)? Or that, having lived on and by it all her long life, she would get so hopelessly lost, in daylight, on the heath?* It seems improbable unless, as is quite possible (something reinforced by her rambling thoughts), she is losing her wits in age. When she sees the boy on her hot journey across the heath, she speaks 'as one in a mesmeric sleep', dazed, that is. However implausible psychologically, her ignorance of what would normally be 'neighbourhood' reinforces the sense that Egdon is a world in itself, cut off entirely from the larger ('real') world.

4/18 *Why did Eustacia not open the door to her mother-in-law, a cruelty from which so much suffering subsequently springs?* Because, when the old lady comes to the house, Wildeve is in the house (as is a sleeping Clym). Wildeve offers to go into the other room. But, apparently in a dilemma, Eustacia is frozen—suspecting that the knocking may have woken Clym (his mother's rapping on the door, loud as it is, does not in fact wake him, so exhausted is he by his physical labour). By the time Eustacia has bundled Wildeve out of the house by the back door, a rejected Mrs Yeobright has left the front door—although it is hard to think that in the heat, and feeble as she is, she can be far off when Eustacia has got things straight. The narrative explains that Mrs Yeobright's path 'lay hidden from Eustacia by a shoulder of the hill'. This it is that renders the old lady invisible when Eustacia opens the door. As so often in Hardy, there is a malign concatenation of mischance. Typically, Eustacia feels no guilt, blaming it all on 'some indistinct, colossal Prince of the World, who had framed her situation and ruled her lot'. (None the less, the narrative adds: 'but nothing could save her from censure in refusing to answer at the first knock'.) Wildeve feels no responsibility, although it is his reck-lessness (or worse) which is, ultimately, to blame. Clym (although wholly innocent in the matter) feels guilty to a life-threatening degree. It is hardly, however, as Clym wrongly insists, tantamount to murder.

4/19 *What is Tamsie's 'illness' as she calls it talking to her cousin Clym?* The fact that she is eight months pregnant. Since, as she later says (by reference to Guy Fawkes day), the baby is born in early September, the child must have been conceived (i.e the illness contracted) practically on the night of her wedding to Wildeve.

4/20 *Where has Diggory Venn been on his long stay away—during which the crisis between the Yeobrights happens?* We never know. It cannot be his arranging the purchase of his dairy farm, which is in the neighbourhood, eight miles away. In this novel, characters often seem oddly ignorant of things happening only a couple of miles distant. There seems also to be a kind of truce in his 'silent system' vendetta against Wildeve. Possibly Diggory's circuit of reddle-customers sometimes takes him far afield.

4/21 *Why does Susan Nunsuch firmly believe that Eustacia is a witch?* Simply the lady's solitariness, that she has raven black hair, wears cloaks, and the fact that her (Susan's) son Johnny is unaccountably ill, and that Eustacia is the nearest woman in the neighbourhood who could be a witch. But how ill is Johnny? It appears he is fit enough to go whortleberry picking on the heath, as he is doing when he meets Mrs Yeobright—and he can gather the fruit almost in the front garden of the 'witch's' house which, surely, his superstitious mother would have forbidden him to go anywhere near. Is Johnny really ill, or merely entranced, spell-struck—obsessed with the lady with black hair, as her groom Charley is obsessed? Hardy rather toys with the idea that Eustacia may indeed be a witch, with such comments as her having cast a 'spell' over Wildeve. One of the 'tests' for witches was that, when thrown in water, they float (the element rejecting their wicked-ness). By this criterion Eustacia is clearly not a witch.

4/22 *It is Johnny Nunsuch who tells Clym the terrible truth of what happened when his mother came to Alderworth. Are there any dubious aspects to Johnny's testimony?* It is odd that he and Mrs Yeobright encounter each other in the hollow called 'Devil's Bellows' (pre-sumably from the sound the wind makes) which is out of the line of sight of the house. Mrs Yeobright is, evidently, out of the sight-line of Eustacia when she comes on 'a little boy gathering whortleberries' (Johnny). Yet Johnny claims to have picked up such details as 'the lady with black hair looked out of the side window at her'. He must, presumably, have been spying rather than fruit-picking. One would like to interrogate the young man rather more fully.

4/23 *When he ransacks Eustacia's writing desk, Clym finds nothing incriminating except an empty envelope 'directed to her and the handwriting was Wildeve's'. How does he know Wildeve's handwrit-ing, having been away from the area for so long?* It is mysterious, unless Wildeve puts his name on the envelope which would, pre-sumably, have been delivered by hand. But, prudent lover that he is, Damon would surely be discreet about such things.

4/24 *In justification for her behaviour as a wife, Eustacia tells her infuriated husband (who has discovered the truth of the locked door, as he thinks), 'All persons of refinement have been scared away from me since I sank into the mire of marriage.' Whom is she thinking of?* There are no such persons of quality we see her consorting with, either before or after she becomes Eustacia Yeobright. Are there 'persons of refinement' in the environs of Egdon? Ponies and furze-cutters in plenty, but nothing that one would call 'society'. Eustacia seems, in her distress, to be thinking back to her great days as the queen of Budmouth.

4/25 *Why does Hardy show us so little of the married life of Thomasin and Damon?* It is odd, since we are given a fuller account of the married life of the Yeobrights. The only details we have (his touching Tamsie's face, as one might a pet) suggest no brutality. But he is chronically secretive, which arouses in her irrepressible suspicions—hardening into the quite correct guess that he is running away. Her immediate pregnancy and the concomitant celibacy may, perhaps, have stimulated his appetite, which in turn led to his renewed attentions to Eustacia. But Thomasin remains wraith-like, inscrutable, and leaves a faint impression on the narrative. Does she serve in the inn? Is she the embodiment (she could well be) of the quiet woman herself?

The Mayor of Casterbridge

Level One

1/1 *What, in his Preface to the novel, does Hardy identify as the principal event determining the nineteenth-century history of his native region, 'Wessex'?* The repeal of the Corn Laws (i.e. protectionism for Britain's grain farmers). The repeal of the protectionist tariffs by Peel's government in the sacred cause of 'Free Trade' opened the way to the importation of cheap cereals from the New World where, ironically, Farfrae is (by fate) prevented from going (later, Henchard is also prevented from emigrating to the prairies. Fate again). Peel's reform had catastrophic effects on the south-west of England, the country's 'bread basket'. The economy of Casterbridge, as depicted in the novel, is clearly pre-Corn Law Repeal, with harvests, for example, wholly dependent on capricious weather conditions. But the imminent (political) change is felt, like a change in the weather. It is odd that no one in Casterbridge (a town deposited in a county-sized corn-field) seems ever to discuss politics, free trade, or the agricultural interest. It is a community thick with history, but with no current politics. Why is the local MP not looking after his constituency's interests, invested as they are in the grain-producing trade? Why is the Mayor not agitated?

1/2 *When does the action open?* 'Before the nineteenth century had reached one-third of its span'. That is, one may calculate, before 1833. This loose chronological framing would put the opening scene of the novel in the troubled and economically distressed 1820s, which perhaps explains why Henchard has been unable to secure fixed work for himself in the 'fodder' line, and has been reduced to vagrant and seasonal hay-trussing. The sale of Susan takes place on 15 September, after the Wessex fields have been harvested (which explains why Henchard has money in his purse to squander on Mrs Goodenough's rum). When

Elizabeth-Jane looks at the blacklined card announcing Newson's death, however, the date is given as '184–'. Since Elizabeth-Jane is 'around eighteen', the main action may be assumed to be in the middle years of that decade. Hardy is more precise about historical period than in some other of his major novels.

1/3 *How old is Henchard, when he makes his great oath, and how old is he when he is reunited with his family?* He married at eighteen. Susan says they have been married a couple of years. Henchard is, presumably, still the right side of forty.

1/4 *At which season of the year do Susan and Elizabeth-Jane return to Weydon Priors?* September. The same month that the wife-sale occurred, and—with the harvest gathered in, the season of celebratory fairs and country fêtes. As ye reap, so shall ye sow.

1/5 *What is Henchard's dental state in middle age?* He has 'thirty-two sound white teeth'. Clean and sound teeth, in Victorian England, were something of a rarity. Dentistry for workers of Henchard's class would, probably, be only available at fairs (as 'tooth-pulling'), along with the furmity.

1/6 *How long has the regenerate Henchard been sober when Susan sees him again?* Nineteen years exactly, when she and Elizabeth-Jane return in 'September 184–'. This, of course, would make the 'around eighteen' which Elizabeth-Jane is described as being slightly (but significantly) too young for her to be Henchard's daughter. It seems strange that he never, in all the years she lives with him, enquires closely about her age, or notices that her birthday is different (as it certainly must be) from that of 'his' Elizabeth-Jane. The practice of commemoratively naming a child after a dead sibling was common in the nineteenth century and would not, one imagines, have struck contemporary readers as an unlikely detail.

1/7 *How does Elizabeth-Jane help pay the bill at the Three Mariners?* By serving in the bar.

1/8 *Where is Farfrae bound for?* Bristol, and then 'the great wheat-growing districts of the West'. Would, for Henchard's sake, that he had achieved this aim.

1/9 *What refreshment does Henchard offer Farfrae, having hired him?* Pigeon pie and ale. A business lunch.

1/10 *What decoratively classical figures flank Henchard's mantel-piece?* Apollo and Diana—divinities associated with love, beauty, and female independence. We first discover the detail as he prepares to divulge the complications of his love-life to Farfrae. They make strange companions to the evangelical texts on his bookshelf. We assume they are a throwback to the Romans, who were once Casterbridge's top people—but less straitlaced in their morality.

1/11 *What is Susan's nickname among the children of the town?* 'The Ghost', which in a sense she is. She is bodiless—wasting away—and has come back to haunt Henchard.

1/12 *What are Lucetta's various names?* Lucette Le Sueur (indicating her 'French extraction'), Lucetta Templeman (indicating her connection with her rich Bristol aunt). The name 'Lucetta' seems to translate as 'little light' (or, perhaps, 'old flame').

1/13 *What was Lucetta's father, by profession, and what kind of childhood did she have?* He was (we are told in passing) an officer in the army and her childhood was passed among garrison towns. 'Bath is where my people really belong to,' she says, mendaciously and rather loftily. Her father perhaps settled in Jersey to avoid creditors. Or possibly scandal.

1/14 *Who says, 'the romance of the sower is gone for good'?* Elizabeth-Jane. She has been reading voraciously, of course—it is not the kind of remark which an untutored country girl might come out with, nor Elizabeth-Jane, a couple of years earlier.

1/15 *What is 'Mr Fall', the astrologer, called behind his back?*

'Wide-oh'—on account of his reputation as a weather-caster. 'Wide' has the association of 'smart', 'clever', 'wide awake'.

1/16 *How much does Henchard pay his waggoners?* Eight shillings a week—a fairly generous wage, we deduce, since the cautious Farfrae (like the proverbially mean Scot) pays a shilling less.

1/17 *Who is the Mayor of Casterbridge, between Henchard's and Farfrae's terms?* Dr Chalkfield, but for less than a year. His term is cut short by death.

1/18 *How did Elizabeth-Jane acquire her 'wonderful skill in netting'?* She picked it up 'in childhood by making seines [fishing nets] in Newson's home'. There is a part of her which is a fisherman's daughter as well as the self-improved woman who can construe Ovid. Her later life will, we can guess, be something of a struggle to detach herself fully from her humble, fisherman's cottage origins.

1/19 *Where does Henchard make his home, after his bankruptcy?* 'Jopp's cottage by the Priory Mill'. Jopp (although it seems rather unlikely) has a couple of rooms to sublet. The priory, of course, is a ruined building—ruined, as is Henchard.

1/20 *What is Henchard's immediate plan, after being ruined?* To emigrate to the New World—as once was Farfrae's ambition, he ironically notes. Why doesn't he leave? Because Elizabeth-Jane visits and begins to care for him, renewing his sense that he belongs in Casterbridge. Nor, of course, can he flee his destiny any more than Oedipus (whose tragic career is often alluded to in Hardy's novel).

1/21 *What, in his working clothes, does the ruined Henchard wear on his head?* A 'rusty silk hat', a relic from his great days as mayor and businessman. It is hard for the reader to picture, but necessary if one is to apprehend the grotesque pathos of the man's condition.

1/22 *Where do Casterbridge's unfortunates (the* misérables *of the town, as Hardy calls them, with an allusion to Victor Hugo) like to gather, despondently?* At one of the town's two bridges, the more shameless *misérables* on the brick structure nearer the public way, those less wretched on the older stone bridge beyond it (which, presumably, gave the town its name). The stone bridge is a favourite resort of suicides.

1/23 *When was the last skimmity-ride in Casterbridge?* 'Ten years ago, if a day', according to the ghoulish Mrs Cuxom. Time for another, is the implication.

1/24 *Who looks after Henchard in his last days, and why?* Abel Whittle, because he was 'kind-like to mother'. Good deeds, like bad deeds, have their consequences.

1/25 *What does Henchard die of?* Starvation, like the bird he gives his 'daughter' as a wedding present.

Level Two

2/1 *Who is the 'Mayor of Casterbridge' referred to in Hardy's title?* Automatically the reader responds 'Michael Henchard'. But, for the greater part of the narrative, Casterbridge's gilt chain of office hangs round the neck of Farfrae. And there is an intervening holder of the office, Dr Chalkfield (of whom we know very little other than that he is briefly mayor and dies), between the principal antagonists. A more pedantic Hardy might have called the novel 'The Mayorship of Casterbridge'.

2/2 *What is 'almost the only attraction' of Susan's face?* 'Mobility'. Ironic, since mobility—moving from place to place—will be Susan's destiny in life. The term also suggests a certain quickness of temper: evident, for example, in her accepting, in an apparent spasm of anger, her husband's offer to sell her and her daughter off to a stranger.

2/3 *Why does Henchard go to Mrs Goodenough's ill-fated furmity tent?* Because, mistakenly, his wife wants to prevent him going to the beer tent—thinking that non-alcoholic furmity (a kind of fruity cordial) will keep him safe from indulging his weakness for strong liquor—something already known to her.

2/4 *What two-winged creatures fly through, or around, the furmity tent?* A swallow, while the booth is open, symbolizing flight and the shortness of life; and a bluebottle, as Henchard recovers, a living corpse, from the worst hangover of his life.

2/5 *What plague, as in Thebes under Oedipus' reign, afflicts Caster-bridge under Henchard's mayoral rule?* Blighted wheat, and bread flat as a 'toad' and as unpalatable to the Casterbridge taste as sliced toad.

2/6 *Where, according to Solomon Longways, does Michael Henchard 'go wrong'?* By going into 'other things' than 'dealing in wheat, barley, oats, hay, roots, and such-like'. We gather that Henchard has already embarked on the bad business practices that will eventually ruin him. What these other things are (property, livestock, dairy produce?) we never precisely know.

2/7 *Why does Farfrae stay at the Three Mariners rather than the King's Arms? And why does Susan tell her daughter they 'must' stay there?* Farfrae lodges at the inn because it is more 'moderate'. Cheaper, that is, than the King's Arms, the most fashionable of Casterbridge's hostelries. Susan and Elizabeth-Jane stay at the Three Mariners because, as Elizabeth-Jane says, 'we must be respectable'. Hardy is noticeably nostalgic about the Three Mariners, its crazy antique aspect and stately host, Stannidge, and 'a secondary set of worthies'. The hostelry has, he laments, since been pulled down. The ale is of 'twelve bushel strength'. This alludes not merely to the potency of the brew, but also to the green bush hung outside traditional ale houses to indicate that there was a fresh brew.

2/8 *Does Henchard break his word to Jopp, on the matter of employing him?* Yes. The arrangement was that Jopp could come 'Thursday or Saturday'. He comes (from Jersey) on the second of those dates—only to be told that it is too late.

2/9 *How much money does Henchard, with afterthought, give Elizabeth-Jane to take back to Susan?* Five guineas, her purchase price all those years ago at Weydon Priors.

2/10 *Where does Henchard arrange to meet Susan, after he learns that she has come to Casterbridge?* The 'Ring', recollecting what she threw at him, on their parting nineteen years before. What, one wonders, happened to the wedding ring? Did Newson give her another, and is she still wearing Newson's ring when she arrives, as a respectable 'widow', at Casterbridge? Landladies (see *Jude*) would notice such details.

2/11 *Wherein, as a corn-factor, lie Farfrae's skills?* He is good with the 'books'—'finnikin details', as the less finicky Henchard thinks them. He has a talent for 'ciphering and mensuration'. Farfrae represents the bureaucratic efficiencies which, despite his slender five foot nine inch frame, will enable him to outdo his more muscular, less cerebral, predecessor as mayor and chief corn-factor in Casterbridge. One order replaces another.

2/12 *Where does Lucetta's only living relative live?* Bristol. The relative is rich. Lucetta is, apparently, her only living relative although there is no intimacy nor, we suspect, moral approval on the aunt's part.

2/13 *Who is characterized by 'honesty in dishonesty'?* Susan, although it would seem more generous to see her as one of Hardy's cast of 'simpletons'.

2/14 *What work task does Nance Mockridge carry out in Henchard's yard?* She wimbles hay-bonds—that is, she intertwines hay into the strings that will bind the bundles, or stooks. There is, presumably, an allusion to the Three Fates; one spins, one weaves, one cuts.

2/15 *How long does the mayor hold office in Casterbridge, and what promotion thereafter is denied Henchard?* The mayor has two years' tenure only. Because, after the arrival of his wife and Farfrae, there is 'something in the air that changed his luck', Henchard is denied elevation to the rank of alderman, the 'Peerage of burghers' in the municipal hierarchy.

2/16 *What dialect word in Elizabeth-Jane's mouth most vexes her 'father'?* 'Leery'—that is, she feels 'strange' after her walk in the churchyard. It may be her walking in the churchyard (where her mother's grave is) which annoys Henchard.

2/17 *What is 'ladies' hand'?* The woman's decorative style of handwriting, distinct from the functional calligraphy of 'clerks' hand' (copperplate), which men like Farfrae would use.

2/18 *How many years does the judicious (and straight-talking) Elizabeth-Jane reckon her mistress, Lucetta, has before she becomes 'hopelessly plain'?* 'It may be five years . . . Or, with a quiet life, as many as ten. With no love you might calculate on ten.' Love, Elizabeth-Jane rightly observes, wears a woman out terribly.

2/19 *What, for those with an eye on the harvest, is the weather like in June, as Henchard's fortunes progressively fail?* Unfavourable. In early August, it is excellent. Then, on the eve of harvest, the weather dampens, like a 'damp flannel' to the face. This perverse meteorological sequence ruins Henchard, who is impulsively induced to buy, store, and sell at exactly the wrong time for the market. The unpredictability of the English growing and harvesting season is one reason why it will, in a very few years, lose out to the prairies of the New World with their reliable climate.

2/20 *Why does Henchard (in the scene of Lucetta's fainting under the pressure of having to accept his proposal) call Elizabeth-Jane a* *'no'thern [northern] simpleton'*? Possibly she was brought up substantially (having returned from America) in some northern coastal port. Hardy never precisely tells us what the young woman's accent is (before, that is, being overlaid by genteel company and rigorous self-improvement).

2/21 *By what right is Henchard a magistrate at petty sessions?* By right of 'his late position as mayor'—he holds his place on the magistrate's bench for one year only. Unluckily for him, as it transpires.

2/22 *Who is Henchard's 'great creditor' in his time of financial distress, and why cannot Lucetta intercede with him?* 'Grower' (the name suggests he is a farmer, in the corn business, whose crop Henchard bought; now he finds himself unable to settle up). Lucetta cannot intercede because Grower 'was a witness' at her secret wedding to Farfrae. By accident, Grower happened to be in Port-Bredy at the time.

2/23 *How creditable, or credible, is Elizabeth-Jane's self-education?* More creditable, perhaps, than credible. Some few months after being in Lucetta's house she is construing Ovid. A remarkable feat for a girl who, a little while earlier, was mending fishing nets.

2/24 *What, according to Abel Whittle, is the advantage and what the disadvantage of being employed by Farfrae rather than Henchard?* 'We work harder, but we bain't made afeard now.' They also get a shilling a week less.

2/25 *What strange headgear (but indicative of where he has come from) does Newson have, when he comes to Casterbridge?* 'A cap of sealskin'—a maritime souvenir from Canada, one assumes, and perhaps a clue as to where he has come by his new wealth: seal hunting.

Level Three

3/1 *Is there anything to be made of the fact that Michael Henchard has never tasted furmity, while Susan has, often, as we gather?* He may, unlike her, not originally have come from Wessex. She is described as a 'peasant'. He has a dead brother, we learn. Otherwise, Henchard's origins are entirely obscure.

3/2 *Is Henchard's hiring Farfrae 'destiny' working its vengeful way with him, or is it to be ascribed to a defect in his chronically self-destructive 'character' (as the subtitle to the novel cues us)?* Susan, who has known Michael best, asserts the second. Hiring Farfrae (after he has, effectively, hired someone else for the post) is in line with his 'impulsiveness'; a quality that is both a strength (in business) and a weakness (in personal relationships).

3/3 *What books does Henchard prominently display in his living room?* A 'Family Bible' (what names, one wonders, are inscribed on the inside fly leaf?), a 'Josephus' (a history of Judaea under the Romans, like Casterbridge an outpost of the empire), and a 'Whole Duty of Man'. Are the books there as decor, or do they give some insight into the stern, Old Testament, morality which Henchard applies to the moral dilemmas of his life?

3/4 *'Casterbridge', the narrator tells us, 'announced old Rome in every street'. What can one read into this antiquarian observation, if anything?* Rome brings with it associations of violence, of gladiatorial combat, of the fall of empires (even those as small as those based on the corn trade), and of paganism.

3/5 *What official post, in addition to mayor, does Henchard occupy?* He is a churchwarden. The same church, one assumes, in whose precincts Mrs Goodenough publicly urinates (Henchard's offence is more private—but morally of the same kind).

3/6 *Who are the principal adulterers in the novel?* Henchard, we assume, has had carnal relations with Lucetta. And Susan—from the strictly legal point of view—has, of course, misconducted herself with Newson. Given the divorce law at this period, Henchard could, if he were insane enough, bring a successful suit against Susan on the grounds of her long and improper liaison with Newson. She could not, however, divorce him for his dalliance with Lucetta.

3/7 *Where and how does Newson 'die'?* On the 'Newfoundland trade'—cod fishing on the Grand Bank there. Trawling was introduced in the 1840s. Newson and Susan tried Canada but are, like the Donns in *Jude the Obscure*, back-migrants. He 'dies' off the Canadian coast—swept overboard with other sailors. A false report of death ensues. Given the fact that steam power was just coming along, and with it rapid communication, Newson could certainly have got word back to Susan that he was still alive. But, as he later says, he thought it would be a 'kindness' to her (she having been disabused about the legality of wife-sale) to leave her in ignorance of his having survived. (But why did he not feel the need to send the poor woman and his child money? Was that 'kindness'?) Disencumbered of Susan (who seems something of a jinx to the men in her life), Newson evidently—like Henchard—thrives. A humble and penurious seaman when we first meet him, he is, at his daughter's wedding, 'a merchant captain'. We can put together little of the life the so-called Newson family lived before his 'death', except that Susan (who must be very simple) believed the wife-sale (not unknown in the early nineteenth century) to be legally binding until disabused on the matter by well- or ill-meaning friends with a better grasp of English law than she. Elizabeth-Jane, we are told, became dextrous mending her father's nets, so presumably he had a small coastal vessel of his own, before becoming a seaman on a deep-sea trawler. Very late in the narrative, when Newson returns, he says that the three lived for some time in 'America' (Canada)—although Elizabeth-Jane never mentions that she has seen so much of the world.

3/8 *What is the great 'national event', the occasion of the fête, which* *brings about the breakdown in the Henchard–Farfrae partnership?* It is unclear whether it is the royal wedding between Albert and Victoria (1841) or the birth of some royal infant. The event reminds the reader that the Victorian era, with its severer morality (especially in matters marital), is looming. The times will not be propitious for wife-sellers and adulterers like Henchard.

3/9 *Why does Farfrae stay in Casterbridge as a corn and hay merchant after Henchard has discharged him? Why not, as he originally intended, travel on?* His heart may, unusually for him, have some sway over his canny Scottish head. He has seen a woman, perhaps two indeed, that he may want to marry. Farfrae has also, while in his rival's employ, learned the secrets and weaknesses of Michael Henchard's business and built up a client list. He is not starting from scratch.

3/10 *Under what circumstances does Michael Henchard descend from standard English into dialect?* Rage, principally. See, for instance, his furious comment on learning that Farfrae is setting up as his trade rival: 'if I can't overbid such a stripling as he, then I'm not wo'th a varden ['farthing']!' When he is composed, Henchard speaks a heavily correct English. How, one wonders, did he pick up this skill? He is naturally intelligent, but one suspects that he imposed on himself a rigorous course of 'self-improvement' when he came to Casterbridge. Samuel Smiles would have approved.

3/11 *What does Susan ordain should be used as weights to close her eyelids, when her body is laid out for burial, and what happens to the weights?* Her eyes are sealed by four ounce-pennies, in two linen bags, later buried in the garden. Christopher Coney (the 'cannibal') digs them up and spends the coins at the Three Mariners. Nothing can remain buried in Casterbridge—particularly not past scandals.

3/12 *Is Elizabeth-Jane illegitimate?* Legally she is.

3/13 *What do unruly boys do to the stone mask which embellishes the* *outside gate to High-Place Hall?* They hurl stones at it, giving the smiling face a pock-marked, syphilitic look. One recalls the punitive stones thrown at the woman taken in adultery—something that will be Lucetta's fate.

3/14 *Hardy says that the mechanical horse drill 'created about as much sensation in the corn-market as a flying machine would create at Charing Cross'. What flying machines is he thinking of?* Not, in the mid-1880s, aeroplanes. It is still a good decade and a bit until Kitty Hawk. One supposes that Hardy is indulging in a piece of uncharacteristic science fiction here—something along the lines of 'pigs might fly' and so one day (ho, ho) might carts.

3/15 *Why does Mrs Goodenough come to Casterbridge?* We are never told. It is, presumably, another example of the malign magnetism that pulls the characters towards disaster.

3/16 *What work does Henchard accept, after his ruin?* He applies for the position of journeyman hay-trusser, with Farfrae. Not only is it day work, it is also seasonal. It is, presumably, September again. A little later we learn that he works until six in the evening (when, presumably, dusk falls) but that it is cool enough to warrant a fire, into which he throws Lucetta's injudicious letter, after he has insulted her in Farfrae's yard. It is light shortly after five in the morning. All this points to September, when bad things always happen to the hero.

3/17 *Which psalm does the poker-wielding Henchard demand the terrified church band play for him, as they take their refreshment in the inn, and why does Henchard choose that one?* 'Psalm the hundred-and-ninth, to the tune of *Wiltshire*'. It is appropriate because of its damnatory sentiments: 'His seed shall orphans be, his wife | A widow plunged in grief, etc.'

3/18 *What happened to Archibald Leith?* He was one of Farfrae's friends, and was murdered. That is all we know of the man. It is the most peripheral of details, at the faded edge of the narrative.

But the violence suggests to the curious mind a possible reason for Farfrae's leaving Scotland and his manifest disinclination to return.

3/19 *What is the occasion of Farfrae being prematurely made mayor?* The death of Dr Chalkfield, in office. It forestalls the plan which he and Lucetta have half-formed of leaving Casterbridge. Fatefully, they now stay to play the tragedy out to its end.

3/20 *Who pays for the skimmity ride?* Newson. He pitches in a sovereign to 'see the old custom', not knowing what trouble he is financing. The sovereign also indicates that he has worked his way back and is flush with money. On his second visit to Casterbridge, he is identified as a 'merchant captain'. How, one wonders, does he know that Susan had come to Casterbridge? He says he was told, but by whom? Surely Susan would have kept it to herself.

3/21 *Who is the doctor who replaces the unfortunate Dr Chalkfield?* Dr Bath, which presumably is where he originally came from. Bath, with its spa and ancient, wealthy, and valetudinarian population, was famous for its doctors. Casterbridge is evidently coming up in the world. Bath may be to Chalkfield (a name with local Wessex overtones) what Farfrae is to Henchard.

3/22 *Who likes to see 'the trimming pulled off Christmas candles' (i.e. the high and mighty of Casterbridge brought low)?* Nance Mockridge; the spiteful shrew.

3/23 *When he treats Lucetta, prostrate after witnessing the skimmity ride, the doctor observes 'a fit in the present state of her health means mischief'. What is the present state of her health?* She is somewhat wasted, but the clear implication is that she is pregnant and will miscarry. This is later confirmed.

3/24 *Where does Henchard see his 'body', and what bodies normally float there?* He sees the effigy of himself, thrown away after the skimmity ride, floating in Ten-Hatches-Hole, on the Blackwater stream, Casterbridge's favourite jumping-off point for suicides.

3/25 *How many times does Newson visit Casterbridge, before being reunited with his daughter?* Twice. The first time he was ignorant of Henchard's presence there, the second he was fobbed off with the cruel lie that his 'wife' and daughter were dead.

Level Four

4/1 *What, since the novel's action stops around the late 1840s, can we foresee (from historical events known to us) to be the subsequent history of the surviving characters?* Ironically, with the collapse of the Wessex corn trade after 1846, it will probably not be long before Farfrae is also ruined—if less tragically than Henchard, since he will certainly have prudently saved a portion of his wealth, and has Lucetta's inheritance to cushion his fall. One order replaces another. A blight will fall on Casterbridge's corn that not even the Scotsman's expertise can cure.

4/2 *Is Henchard what we (but not Hardy) would call an alcoholic?* He seems to be—he can only forbear from drink by violent abstinence and what, in Alcoholics Anonymous, is called 'the geographical cure' (i.e. moving to a new place where one can start over again). The prognosis for the 'geographical' is not, according to AA orthodoxy, good. It is telling that when he makes his great oath Henchard does not swear to give up drink for ever. Practising alcoholics typically give themselves escape clauses of this kind. If he is an alcoholic—that is, the victim of a 'disease'—his great crime is mitigated (as twentieth-century apologists might argue). It wasn't Michael who sold Susan but John Barleycorn.

4/3 *What is Farfrae doing so far from ('far frae') home?* The Scotsman's motive for abandoning his 'ain countree' is, we apprehend, agricultural distress in Scotland (his house, we learn much later, was pulled down 'for improvements'). He comes from 'near Edinboro'' and, as far as we can work out, has no close relatives—no one, for example, comes down for either of his weddings; the only guest of honour is the returned Newson. Despite his sentimental crooning, Farfrae seems to have no love for his native Scotland ('I don't want to go back!' he tells Elizabeth-Jane, forcefully). Why, however, he should be passing through Wessex (as opposed to taking a shorter trip to Glasgow, or Liverpool—major transatlantic ports) is mysterious. It is not a direct route to Bristol, as there is, at the time he comes to the town, no railway at Casterbridge.

4/4 *Hardy daringly tantalizes the reader with a huge nineteen-year hiatus, during which, we are to understand, a humble journeyman hay-trusser becomes the most important personage and dynamic businessman in Casterbridge. How does Henchard achieve this success in life?* There is an un-narrated novel enclosed in the white space blanking out these two decades. Casterbridge must, one assumes, have had corn-factors doing business before the arrival of Michael Henchard. Nor, with only Newson's five guineas in his pocket, can the hay-trusser have had capital enough to set himself up, or buy himself into the trade. He presumably worked his way to the top by his 'one talent of energy'. Would he have risen to the top had he found the absconded Susan and his daughter the morning after he 'sold' them? Probably not. Workmen, like Abel Whittle, presumably worked for Henchard's predecessor. And, from the mixed brutality and seigneurial kindness with which he treats the luckless Abel, we can guess at the qualities which enabled Henchard, the 'New Man' (before the newer Farfrae appeared), to succeed. Henchard, we are told, has no mastery of 'ledgers' and relies on 'viva voce techniques' and rules of thumb—or rules of fist and muscled arm. In the long view, of course, Henchard has merely cleared the ground, by his slash and burn techniques, for the bureaucrats of the corn trade, like Farfrae.

4/5 *Christopher Coney enquires, sensibly enough, why Farfrae has left his 'ain countree' if 'ye be so wownded about it'. Why indeed?* We may assume that the drift towards sheep farming, following the

Scottish clearances earlier in the century, has given the young Scot no opportunity to practise his skills as a cereal trader. For someone as rooted to his region as firmly as Hardy, this propensity to voluntary exile in Farfrae may suggest some moral criticism.

4/6 *According to Buzzford the dealer, 'Casterbridge is a old hoary place o' wickedness, by all account.' What, exactly, is this legacy of 'wickedness'?* As Buzzford compiles it, in his mélange of the Monmouth Rebellion of 1688 and the Roman occupation: ' 'Tis recorded in history that we rebelled against the king one or two hundred years ago, in the time of the Romans, and that lots of us was hanged on Gallows-Hill, and quartered, and our different jints sent about the country like butcher's meat'. Judge Jeffreys, and the savage Roman Governor, have left their bloody signatures on Casterbridge.

4/7 *Why does Susan pass off Newson's daughter as Henchard's daughter?* It is the cause of tragedy: unintendedly. There may be some lingering resentment against the husband who treated her so shamefully—she wants to turn the knife, pay him out. But given Susan's simple honesty (she initially believes, astoundingly, that Newson is legally her partner), one presumes that she deceives Henchard against her better nature, in order to apply pressure on him to take her back—which he might not do if she were encumbered with a bastard. Would she ever have told Henchard the truth, had she lived? Presumably not.

4/8 *Henchard tells Farfrae that he is 'something of a woman hater'. Has he contrived to keep himself 'pure' (as well as dry) during the nineteen years of his abstinence?* We assume, from later complications of the plot, and the description of his trips to Jersey, that he has not. Sexual abstinence was not, of course, a clause in his great oath.

4/9 *Why has it been Henchard's custom to 'run across to Jersey'?* It is his business practice to visit 'in the way of business, particularly in the potato and root season'. Ostensibly, he would go in spring to get the new potato crop, which will have come to ripeness earlier than on the colder mainland, a few miles to the north. But, clearly, it is oats as much as roots, which he seeks in foreign parts. It would not do for the mayor (and a churchwarden to boot) to dally with female company in Casterbridge or its neighbourhood. Nor, since he is still (as he knows) married, can he honestly pay court to a Casterbridge lady. Oddly, Henchard's position is strangely like that of Rochester in *Jane Eyre*. He is (we plausibly suspect) a strongly sexed man forced—by reason of a hidden wife—to live the life of a monk. Twenty-one years without alcohol is one thing. That many years without the solace of female companionship is something quite other. There are a number of hints (not least his sacrificing his promising career in the fodder business by marrying at eighteen) that Henchard has a strong sexual appetite.

4/10 *What did Henchard fall ill of in Jersey?* The illness may, to indulge speculation, have been a convenient fiction. It would have been devised to explain why he should have had a lady in a boarding house visiting his bedroom at all hours. 'We got naturally intimate,' Henchard says. A highly sexed man, a beautiful woman, a bed—the old story. But if this is the case, why would Henchard feel obliged to maintain the fiction to Farfrae? Unless, of course, he apprehended a vein of strict Scottish morality in the young man.

4/11 *How, as the local Jersey gossips think, has Lucetta behaved 'scandalously'?* They had been, as Henchard says, 'careless of appearances'. He therefore, as he tells Farfrae, offered to marry her. The whole story seems unlikely—particularly this last detail. It is inconceivable that Henchard would take the risk of committing bigamy, with all the sworn lies and dangerous criminality the act would entail. His name is too well known. This raises the interesting question of why, when he moved to Casterbridge, Henchard did not change his name, as he easily could have. He is, one assumes, not telling Farfrae the whole, humiliating truth of the matter of his involvement with Lucetta. The likelihood is that he offered to make her his mistress, with a cover story for local consumption in Jersey that she was his wife. A simpler explanation, perhaps, is that Henchard (and, less willingly, Lucetta) were victims of early Victorian standards.

4/12 *Why does Elizabeth-Jane not recognize her mother's handwriting in the letter summoning her to a meeting with Farfrae?* It is odd that she doesn't. Presumably Susan disguised her hand, but for someone semi-literate that trick is not easily performed. Perhaps she persuaded a servant to write the note for her.

4/13 *Is it plausible that Lucetta (the mysterious 'lady') could be as unknown to Elizabeth-Jane as she is, given the smallness of Casterbridge? And could this rich visitor to the town have bought High-Place Hall without Henchard's knowing all about it? Or* something *about it?* One assumes that the ostracism (compounded by his natural hauteur) has kept Henchard in ignorance as to what is going on a few hundred yards away.

4/14 *Why does Lucetta choose to settle in Casterbridge?* It seems to be a function of the strangely malignant magnetism (Sophoclean fate), which draws all the characters to their doomed collision. Or possibly she intended a little torment of her tormentor, now that she is rich, independent, and 'respectable' again. As time, and her initial infatuation, pass it is not clear that her motive is to marry Henchard as it initially was, which makes her decision to stay enigmatic. Hardy frequently declines to investigate too far into the mysteries of the female mind.

4/15 *What (despite her former prejudices) makes Lucetta amenable (almost at first sight) to the attentions of a 'tradesman' like Farfrae?* Her 'ups-and-downs, capped by her indiscretions with Henchard'.

4/16 *Who is 'the only one in Casterbridge' who knew that Lucetta 'came truly from Jersey' (not, as she claims, Bath)?* The villainous Jopp. He 'often' saw Henchard on the island. But did he know of the 'scandal'? Surely, if it was so notorious, he would have picked up some of the gossip (Hardy intimates as much in Chapter 36, where he says that Jopp 'knew there had been something of the nature of wooing between Henchard and the now Mrs Farfrae'). And it was presumably on Jersey that Henchard first met Jopp and decided he liked the cut of his jib (until he discovered he liked that of Farfrae better). Why, as an habitué of Mixen Lane, does Jopp not say anything earlier to anyone on the subject of Lucetta's past? Is he, perhaps, contemplating blackmail?

4/17 *How, actually, has Lucetta 'compromised' herself, in her earlier relationship with Henchard?* This is a nagging enigma in the narrative. Something injudiciously sexual, real or suspected, is hinted at—but there seems to be no love child, no *in flagrante delicto* scandal. Nor is any breach of promise suit threatened. Henchard seems not to have been compromised (which may be more a testimony to the ruling double standard in such matters than his impeccable conduct). He has manifestly inspired violently erotic letters from Lucetta, which eventually lead to her death.

4/18 *Where could the furmity woman have, legally, committed her 'nuisance', rather than by the church?* At this date, the only public urinals (*cabinets de convenance*) for women would have been at the railway station. There isn't one at Casterbridge for a few years yet, as we are told. It is, presumably, the shameless display of the act rather than the fact that she relieves herself which constitutes the offence. Discreet urination in public places must be a fact of life in Casterbridge.

4/19 *Why is Henchard content for Elizabeth-Jane to leave his household?* If she is not his daughter, as he has now been told, there is impropriety (of which she is blithely unaware). Is she, one wonders, within the degrees of incest as the daughter of another man, by his common-law wife, a woman who previously happened to be the legal wife of Henchard?

4/20 *Why does Lucetta go back on her pledge to marry Henchard and give herself to another?* Because, as she says, 'I learnt of the rumour that you had—sold your first wife at a fair, like a horse or cow'. If it was a rumour, why did she not check it out? Presumably she wanted to get out of the arrangement in order to marry Farfrae, with whom she had fallen madly in love (such being the fickleness of woman), and seized on the excuse. Henchard has some good reason for resentment against her.

4/21 *Is it plausible that Elizabeth-Jane would not know that her mistress (and by now close friend) was getting married? When, for example, the band has been arranged to play at the reception, vast amounts of food ordered, and the church bells have been ordered to be rung?* The only possible explanation—Elizabeth-Jane being a sharp-eyed girl and intimately close to her mistress—is that Lucetta, aware of her young friend's hopes, has guiltily kept the impending marriage secret.

4/22 *Farfrae, we are told, 'had no suspicion whatever of any antecedents in common between her [Lucetta] and the now journey-man hay-trusser'. He does not, that is, know of the affair on Jersey. Is this likely?* It does seem odd. Farfrae does, presumably, know that Lucetta is from the island, and that Henchard once had a serious entanglement there. Elizabeth-Jane knows the truth. So, it seems, does Jopp. Casterbridge is a remarkably discreet place, in some ways.

4/23 *Does Farfrae really not understand the hurt and injury which Henchard feels and that 'Henchard, a poor man in his employ, was not . . . the Henchard who had ruled him'?* He must be very dull— the more so as he is living in Henchard's former house, and owns his former business. There is something inhuman about Donald Farfrae.

4/24 *Why, with Farfrae at his mercy after their gladiatorial combat, does Henchard not kill his opponent?* Because, as he says, 'no man ever loved another as I did thee at one time . . . I cannot hurt thee.' It is an interesting confirmation of the erotic feeling that Henchard, although he cannot understand it, feels for Donald (what woman can Henchard be said truly to 'love'?). After Farfrae leaves, exhausted, Henchard remains, as the narrative puts it, in a womanly attitude. The fighting is a kind of lovemaking.

4/25 *When told by Henchard that his wife and daughter are dead, why does Newson not want to see their graves, or even ask how it was they died?* This indifference suggests that he may, perhaps, be embarrassed at having left his dependants without support now that he, apparently enriched by his Canadian work, has money. He left Casterbridge and 'had not so much as turned his head'. This indifference may also explain Newson's ostentatiously never bearing any grudge against Henchard. His morality, the narrative informs us, has been made 'tolerant', like other 'rovers and sojourners among strange men and strange moralities'. Arguably, his own morality in leaving the mother of his child penniless has not been entirely impeccable.

The Woodlanders

Level One

1/1 *The first character we are introduced to in the narrative shows himself not to be a local in Hintock by his 'rather finical style of dress'. Who is he?* Barber Percomb, the dandyish hairdresser ('haircutter', as far as Marty is concerned) from Sherton. He has a 'waxen woman' in his window, indicating that he caters for the female customer (the corpse-like effigy also enhances his sinister image). A barber for all seasons, on Saturday nights Percomb shears fieldworkers' locks in the back room of his 'salon'. The name (Percomb = pure comb) is not one of Hardy's more brilliant inventions.

1/2 *Where and how did Mrs Charmond notice that Marty's magnificent mane of hair, her only claim to beauty, 'exactly' matched her own?* At church. Mrs Charmond evidently has other things on her mind than the sermon when attending the local place of worship. The living is probably in her gift—that is, it is she who has the privilege of appointing the vicar. Mrs Charmond has a *droit de seigneur* (as she feels) over everything in her 'manor', including the parishioners' hair.

1/3 *What happened when a parcel of Fitzpiers's books was delivered, by mistake, to the vicarage and opened by the unsuspecting parson's wife?* She opened it and went 'into hysterics ... thinking her husband had turned heathen'. It may be, of course, that the books contained some of the heretical theorizing of Charles Darwin, or worse.

1/4 *How much older than Grace is Giles?* He is twenty-five, she twenty. If she has been away at boarding school for the last few years, he must have fallen in love with little Grace when she was very young indeed. Giles was presumably over some of this period apprenticed to his trade of woodman and cidermaker—or, possibly, he worked in his (deceased) father's business as 'Winterborne and Son'.

1/5 *How long has Grace been away, being 'finished' on the Continent?* A year—presumably something arranged, for a fee, by her boarding school. It must have cost rather more than the 'near a hundred a year' Melbury paid out for her school education in England.

1/6 *Of what does Grace dream, on her first night back at Hintock?* 'Kaleidoscopic dreams of a weird alchemist-surgeon, Grammer Oliver's skeleton, and the face of Giles Winterborne.' Not a happy conjunction for Giles.

1/7 *Does Hintock House stand high or low in the landscape?* Low. The Manor House is in a glen, or hollow—a depressed situation for a depressed occupant. It is an 'edifice built in times when human constitutions were damp-proof'. Mrs Charmond's antipathy to the place (used as she is to warm climates) may not be entirely unreasonable.

1/8 *What are Marty South's 'three headaches'?* 'A rheumatic headache in my poll', brought on by catching cold from losing her protective mane of hair; a sick headache over her eyes; and a 'misery headache in the middle of my brain' (from the knowledge that she will never marry Giles). She has, as she says, just begun life 'in earnest'—that is, with awareness of its full awfulness.

1/9 *Who is Giles's 'trusty man and familiar' (i.e. factotum servant)?* Robert Creedle. He recalls the faithful and comically simpleminded servant Caleb Balderstone in Scott's *The Bride of Lammermoor*, a story of star-crossed love recalled at a number of points in *The Woodlanders*. Hardy conceived himself as a disciple of Scott, the novelist who made the regional novel fashionable.

1/10 *What, according to Mr Melbury, characterizes the distinctive*

Hintock gait? 'The regular Hintock shail and wamble'. A lurching way of walking, one gathers ('to wamble' is to wander aimlessly). There are few hard, even surfaces to walk on in the woodland. And, as Fitzpiers might complain, nowhere for a civilized person to go.

1/11 *How do Melbury's huge timber wagons signal to other road users that a large load is on the road?* Each of the four horses has four bells, 'tuned to scale, so as to form two octaves'—a melodious klaxon. Mrs Charmond's carriage, with which (ominously for him) Giles has a kind of road-rage episode when they meet on the foggy road to Sherton, makes its coming known by the more modern device of headlamps.

1/12 *How does Fitzpiers spend his first Midsummer Eve in Hintock?* Disporting in the open fields, among the newly stacked stooks, with Suke Damson, the betrothed of Tim Tangs—a 'roll in the hay', as the vulgar of a later century would put it. The 'frisky maidens' of the village have gathered for the harvest-time rituals which will vouchsafe them a vision of their future husbands. Suke sees something quite different—her future seducer. Is Suke a 'maiden' when she spends Midsummer night with the doctor, one wonders? Hardy leaves the detail hanging, enigmatically.

1/13 *The maidens' vigil on Midsummer Eve is broken up by a visitation of, as they think, 'Satan pursuing us with his hour-glass'. What have they in fact seen?* The American suitor of Mrs Charmond— and, eventually, her killer. He is, could she but see it, bringing with him the closure of Felice's life. The 'hour-glass' is, in fact, his tall hat tucked under his arm. The aura of death around the (unnamed) future assassin is, indeed, prophetic.

1/14 *What, according to Tangs the elder, would cure Melbury of his obsession with his only child?* 'He ought to have a dozen—that would bring him to reason.' The narrator, one gathers, agrees that Melbury is something of a parental monomaniac.

1/15 *What does Fitzpiers intend doing after marriage?* Buying a practice in fashionable Budmouth (for a downpayment of a massive £750, as we learn). He is not keen to be tied to his in-laws—although Melbury's capital will be necessary in the necessary untying.

1/16 *How does Grace identify the faithless arm, which lets a scantily dressed Suke out of Fitzpiers's house at dawn?* By the dressing-gown, which she saw him wearing (as he slept on the sofa) on their first meeting.

1/17 *What does Tim Tangs, Suke's (dangerous) fiancé, do for a living?* He is part of a top and bottom sawyer team—working with another sawyer (his father), he would saw large logs with a two-handled saw.

1/18 *Why does Fitzpiers decide to put black plaster (rather than skin-coloured plaster) on Mrs Charmond's minor scratch?* 'So that it might catch the eyes of the servants and make his presence appear decidedly necessary'.

1/19 *What does the narrative instruct us is the 'one word' which describes Felice Charmond?* 'Inconsequence'.

1/20 *What adjective describes Suke Damson?* 'Buxom'.

1/21 *What is the name of the frisky horse which (when he mistakes it for torpid Darling) brings Fitzpiers to grief?* Blossom.

1/22 *What does Melbury keep in his 'pilgrim's flask' when he undertakes journeys on horseback of twelve miles or more, and what are the fatal consequences of his flask?* It contains rum. After the concussion of his fall from Blossom, the draughts of rum which Melbury forces down Fitzpiers's throat, far from reviving him, inspire his son-in-law to blackguard Hintock, the Melburys, and his wife Grace. He is, in his dazed intoxication, and riding at night, unaware that he is talking to his increasingly furious father-in-law. He believes his interlocutor is some unknown Good Samaritan. This episode in the narrative rather strains credulity.

1/23 *What mistake in entertaining Grace in Sherton does Giles Winterborne (her suitor once more) make?* He takes her to the commercial tavern, rather than the 'dignified Earl of Wessex' hotel—where Fitzpiers was wont to take his wife.

1/24 *What is the name of Giles's habitation in the woods, after he loses his tenure of the cottages with South's death?* One-Chimney Hut.

1/25 *Who, alone, 'approximated to Winterborne's level of intelligent intercourse with Nature'?* Marty South.

Level Two

2/1 *To what does Percomb shrewdly attribute Marty's reluctance to part with her crowning glory?* 'You've got a lover yourself.' His remark is only half-true. She loves, but is not loved.

2/2 *What, when he was a child, burned a sense of his social degradation into Melbury and fired him with the ambition that his child, at least, should rise to a higher station in life?* As he recalls to John Upjohn and Robert Creedle, 'When I was a boy another boy—the pa'son's son along with a lot of others—asked me "Who dragged Whom round the walls of What?" and I said, "Sam Barret, who dragged his wife in a wheeled chair round the tower when she went to be churched." They laughed at me so much that I went home and couldn't sleep for shame.' They should never, he resolved, laugh at his children. Hardy cunningly insinuates the mispronunciation ('pa'son's son') to remind us that the indelible rusticity of Melbury's accent is still there to mark him as 'underbred'.

2/3 *Why does Marty wear pattens when walking the six miles and back to Sherton-Abbas?* To save her boots from getting worn. Gentlewomen (of whom Marty is not one) wear them to prevent their footwear touching the dirt.

2/4 *Why is Giles 'not a very successful seller either of his trees or of his* *cider', excellent though both are?* His 'habit of speaking his mind' militates against him. Perhaps, one may surmise, he is uneasy about 'trading' and the 'cash nexus' on political grounds. There is the persistent hint throughout the novel that Giles is a socialist (as it happened, the novel was published in the politically troubled year of 1887, the famous year of the great socialist riot in Trafalgar Square). He is given to sotto voce sarcasms against the idle rich, like Charmond and Fitzpiers. 'How can you think so much of that class of people?' he angrily asks Grace, after she has been to the Manor House.

2/5 *What are the faggots, produced in such numbers in the woodland, used for?* Mainly, it seems, for fuel in bakeries—which require intense heat—and for kindling. Possibly, too, for fencing. They also bear witness to the fact that the woodlanders waste nothing.

2/6 *How many candles does Grace use in preparing her toilette for her visit to Mrs Charmond, hopeful as she is that a good impression will lead to employment as the rich woman's companion?* She indulges in a 'six-candle illumination'. It is the 'bare-bough' time of year, and darkness falls early. But candles, even in a household as well provided for as the Melburys', would ordinarily be used sparingly.

2/7 *How has Mrs Charmond come to be the 'Lady of the Manor'?* Her husband, enriched by 'iron' in the north, bought up the property, married a fast woman with a stage background (Mrs Charmond, whose maiden and stage names we never know), died childless, leaving his widow, twenty or thirty years his junior, a life interest in the manor. Which is, of course, of no interest at all to Mrs Charmond. She is twenty-seven or twenty-eight at the time of the novel's main action. Mrs Charmond is a prime example of what Thomas Carlyle called the 'useless aristocracy'—leaders who have lost all sense of their responsibility to lead. Societies, like fish, rot from the head downwards.

2/8 *Why does Mrs Charmond want a companion on her trip to the Mediterranean?* She wishes to write a travel book, but is too idle to put pen to paper, and needs a secretary to take down her observations. The chosen amanuensis will have to be someone with whom she feels 'in sympathy'. Presumably she will also want her grapes peeled.

2/9 *Why does Mrs Charmond, in the event, not employ Grace who is, in every sense, eligible to be her travelling companion and amanuensis?* Because, as the women stand together at a mirror, 'Grace's countenance had the effect of making Mrs Charmond appear more than her full age'. That full age, we later learn, is a mere twenty-seven. Grace is seven years her junior. Indifferent as she is to most things, Mrs Charmond is attentive to her image. She is very rarely seen in the open air during the course of the narrative, doubtless fearing the wear and tear of sunlight on her complexion or that her face will appear to disadvantage in full light.

2/10 *Why does Marty habitually call Giles (who calls her 'Marty') 'Mr Winterborne'?* Because he is her father's employer and, when she fills her father's working shoes, her employer too. Giles, apparently, acquiesces in her deference—unfeeling as we may consider it.

2/11 *What misfortunes befall Grace's 'fashionable attire . . . lately brought home with her from the Continent' at Giles's 'randy-voo'?* The boy who polished the wooden chairs left the oil on them, which stained her dress. Robert Creedle, dumping the stew in the bowl on the dining table, splashes her with gravy. With the gloss of the finishing school on her, these accidents of rural life offend Miss Melbury's father.

2/12 *Under what two (different) misapprehensions does Fitzpiers labour on his first sightings of Grace?* His first misapprehension is that she is the Lady of the Manor, Mrs Charmond. When she comes to his house, and accidentally into his living quarters while he sleeps on his sofa, to plead for Grammer Oliver's brain, he assumes she is a dream vision, the incarnation of his 'ideal' of womanhood. Grace can no more live up to that than she can fill his pockets with gold.

2/13 *What is the significance of John South's death, and how old is he when he dies?* Not only his cottage, but the adjacent properties of Winterborne, are 'lifehold'—in Giles's possession only for as long as South lives. John's hold on life is precarious. He is a prematurely moribund fifty-five at the time of his death (five years the hale Melbury's junior). The householders' ancestors thoughtlessly gave up their freehold in return for renovation of their old and decrepit cottages—on the selfish grounds, presumably, that their distant descendants could make their own arrangements. Giles discovers an escape clause in the contract too late—South dies before the lawyer in Sherton can be consulted.

2/14 *What is John South's monomania and what is Fitzpiers's cure for it?* South fears that the large elm (exactly his age) in front of his cottage will fall and crush him. Fitzpiers orders that the tree be felled (even though it and the timber it will yield belong to Mrs Charmond and she has not given permission). The desperate remedy is fatal. Fitzpiers is evidently a better physician than psychologist. His failed experiment impoverishes Giles, who henceforth goes off to live in a hovel in the woods.

2/15 *What does Mrs Charmond, through her agent, do with the cottages that come into her possession with the death of John South?* She has them pulled down—partly in vengeful chagrin at Winterborne's insolence to her when his wagon obstructed her carriage on its way to Italy (via Sherton). 'Pulling down is always the game,' say the villagers. As is, over these mid-Victorian years, rural depopulation.

2/16 *Who tells Fitzpiers who Grace really is (no lady, but the daughter of the local timber-merchant) and what is the high-born doctor's reaction?* Winterborne informs Fitzpiers. 'How comes he to have a daughter of that sort?' Fitzpiers wonders. 'Won't money do anything?' the radically inclined Winterborne sarcastically retorts.

2/17 *Watching Marty's deftness at barking fallen timber, compared* *with her male co-workers, Fitzpiers notes, 'You seem to have a better instrument than they.'* Is her barking-knife sharper, or finer? No, Marty replies, it's only 'that they've less patience with the twigs, because their time is worth more than mine'. Again, we see a kind of primal feminism in Hardy's portrayal of Marty. Dextrous with her fingers, she would have made a wonderful 'typist girl'. Alas, there is no call for stenographers in Wessex.

2/18 *What happens to the timber that we see cut and hauled off in the course of this novel?* One assumes that a large portion of it is sucked into the huge and rapidly expanding metropolis (Melbury's prosperity is surely founded on more than the needs of the local construction industry). And, as London grows, so the woodlands will shrink.

2/19 *Where does Fitzpiers want to get married, and why?* At a registry office. The reason he gives Grace for wanting a civil rather than a religious ceremony is that the registrar's is 'a quieter, snugger, and more convenient place' than a church. The truth is, of course, that he is ashamed of marrying a mere timber-merchant's daughter and wants no ceremony or publicity.

2/20 *Who was Fitzpiers's landlady, before he married and took up residence with the Melburys? How does his former landlady react to his happy event?* Mrs Cox. She is 'soured' by losing him as a tenant, there being not the 'remotest' chance of getting another as good (i.e. as easy to overcharge). She (probably mendaciously) tells him his professional reputation is sadly diminished by his choice of marriage partner (and, by implication, a new residence which confirms him as a 'kept man'). The general sentiment, she maliciously reports, is that 'He ought to have done better than that.' It confirms the new husband's own corrosive sense of having let himself down by his choice of wife.

2/21 *Where, and how, does Mrs Charmond overturn her carriage?* Driving her 'phaeton', she blunders into the ruin of Winterborne's cottage, mistaking it for her turn. The accident and the (minor) hurt she receives are a small stroke of justice in a generally unjust universe.

2/22 *How old is Melbury?* Sixty. It is a significant detail. Since Grace is twenty, he must have had her by his first wife relatively late in life. Her mother died while Grace was very young and Melbury married his second partner, 'a homespun woman'.

2/23 *What, in the small part she plays in the central love triangle (Felice–Fitzpiers–Grace), is Marty South's 'one card'?* She knows the truth about Mrs Charmond's chignon, her false hair, made from Marty's true hair.

2/24 *Where do Fitzpiers and Felice run away to?* Germany, the country where they first met, years before, as star-crossed lovers. They are evidently not discreet in their adulterous liaison, since Felice is hunted down in Baden by her former, homicidal, lover: the assassin from South Carolina.

2/25 *Who gives Melbury the disastrously wrong information about what the new, 1857, Divorce Act will afford Grace?* Fred Beaucock —'once a promising lawyer's clerk and local dandy', now a drunken ne'er do well. 'Unmarrying', in this day and age, Fred assures Melbury, 'is as easy as marrying'. The intricate details of this Act, whose legal complexities are entirely unappreciated by Beaucock, are spelled out in the endnotes to the OWC edition. The Act created a new court and more open access to divorce for the general population. Divorce under the 1857 Act required not only a husband's adultery but some further offence such as violence, incest, sodomy, or desertion without reasonable cause for over two years. It was, in short, double standards institutionalized. Were he so inclined, for example, Fitzpiers could divorce Grace for having passed a few nights in Winterborne's hut. She cannot divorce him for the most flagrant misconduct with Suke and Felice.

Level Three

3/1 *What do Barber Percomb, Mrs Charmond, and Dr Fitzpiers have in common?* They all prey, like genteel vampires, on the locals: Percomb buys Marty's hair, for two guineas, then sells it for many times that to Mrs Charmond, who has capriciously decided she wants it to decorate her own head. Fitzpiers buys Grammer Oliver's brain for ten pounds.

3/2 *What was the 'trick' that the young Mr Melbury played by which he won his first wife from his friend, Giles Winterborne's father?* We never precisely know. He may, perhaps, have slandered his friend. But it was evidently not so serious a treachery as to render it impossible for Winterborne to stay in Hintock. Nevertheless, his 'happiness was ruined' and his marriage to Giles's mother was 'but a half-hearted business with him'.

3/3 *Why did Melbury go to the trouble of having his daughter Grace 'inoculated for the small-pox', something that is still, ten years later, a wonderful event to the (un-inoculated) locals?* He did not, evidently, want her complexion damaged, lest it frustrate the ambitious marriage plans he secretly, and snobbishly, has for her. With the same hopeful scheme in mind, he also had his daughter's skull read by a phrenologist—whom he takes to be a species of fortune teller. It is a tribute to Grace's innate good sense that she has not been 'spoiled' by her fond father's cosseting.

3/4 *What does Marty hear from within Mrs Charmond's carriage, as she (Marty) is given a lift on the box back from Sherton to Hintock?* 'A gentle oral sound, soft as a breeze.' It is Mrs Charmond yawning, the 'majestic' coachman informs her. The lady finds life in the country so dull. 'So rich, and so powerful, and yet to yawn!' says Marty of the woman wearing her hair, 'Then things don't fay with her any more than with we!' Fitzpiers also, as we learn from Grammer Oliver, is given to yawning. 'Ennui' is the word which, did she but know it, would come to Marty's lips, contemplating these two elegant outsiders in her native woodland—as alien, in their way, as H. G. Wells's Martians.

3/5 *What is it, the narrator informs us, that makes 'life what it is'?* The 'Unfulfilled Intention'. A typically Hardyan formula for fate that apparently does not know its own purposes, but drags humanity along behind it. The phrase reflects the novelist's reading in Schopenhauer and Eduard von Hartmann.

3/6 *With what does Fitzpiers first look at Grace? His naked eye?* No, he quizzes her (unconscious) form through an 'eyeglass'. Presumably a lorgnette, or monocle. His eyes, one presumes, have been weakened by all the midnight reading he does—but the scientist looking at an interesting specimen for his collection is also invoked.

3/7 *What do Mr and Mrs Melbury wear to Giles's 'randy-voo', intended to welcome Grace back as his lover?* Mrs Melbury wears her 'best silk'. Mr Melbury, aware of the class difference between him and Giles, wears his 'secondbest suit' (his very best suit, reeking of camphor and not to be worn more than once or twice in a lifetime, is later taken out of the press for the visit to the House, in which he beseeches Mrs Charmond to stop coquetting with Fitzpiers).

3/8 *What, as he nostalgically reminisces, do we gather was Robert Creedle's favourite public entertainment in the good old days of Wessex?* Hang-fairs—the public jollities surrounding public executions. Like the man-trap, still in use till 1840, a thing of the not-too-distant past for contemporary readers of *The Woodlanders*.

3/9 *What, other than their suit and number markings, do Giles's playing cards have on them?* 'Each card had a great stain in the middle of its back, produced by the touch of generations of damp and excited thumbs now fleshless in the grave.' Such domestic squalor (honest dirt though it be) inspires the faintly disgusted Grace to recollect the 'bevy of sylph-like creatures in muslin' with whom she was consorting a few weeks back. Was she happy at school and abroad? She later says not, but in the early chapters of the novel she seems not entirely sure whether sylphs and muslins might not be preferable to sweaty playing cards, gravy stains, and slugs in the salad.

3/10 *How does Robert mitigate the offensiveness of the slug which, unhappily, was served up with Grace's winter greens, at Giles's unlucky festive supper?* 'He was well boiled—I warrant him well boiled. God forbid that a *live* slug should be seed on any plate of victuals that's served by Robert Creedle.' He is not being ironic.

3/11 *What does Giles rename the mare that he buys for Grace, and what eventually happens to the animal?* 'Darling'. It is an ancient, sedate beast and is eventually ridden by Fitzpiers, a 'second-rate' horseman capable only of handling a lady's mount.

3/12 *Who calls Melbury an 'old buffer' and with what effect?* The angry and rude huntsman applies that opprobrious description when Melbury fails to do the hunt the service of shouting 'View Halloo' when he sees a fox passing by. The insult, from a member of the fox-hunting classes (then, as now, upper crust), opens Melbury's old wounds, leading him to resolve that his daughter must not, after all and despite all promises made, marry Winterborne—she must rise above their (Melbury's and Winterborne's) level in life. 'If a black-coated squire or pa'son had been walking with you instead of me he wouldn't have spoken so.' After the 'buffer' episode he forbids Grace from seeing Giles without his knowledge; a disastrous prohibition, as it turns out.

3/13 *Old Grammer Oliver catches a cold ('my wind-pipe is furred like a flue'). What are the momentous consequences for Grace?* The old woman beseeches Grace to buy back her brain from Fitzpiers. It leads to the couple's first meeting, and eventual marriage—a union based on corpse purchase.

3/14 *What does Fitzpiers feel for the woodland region in which he* *has chosen to pursue his career?* 'Having been of late years a town man, [he] hated the solitary midnight woodland.' Like Mrs Charmond, he finds the region dull, lonely and pointless for a man of refined sensibility and cosmopolitan background like himself. The metropolitan snob is a recurrent *bête noire* in Hardy's fiction.

3/15 *How, ingeniously, does Fitzpiers explain Suke's being at his house at dawn, and how, fortuitously, does Grace later discover that the explanation is a barefaced lie?* The little hoyden, he tells (trusting) Grace, was afflicted with the most terrible toothache during the night, and he was woken from his virtuous couch to pull the offending molar instantly. Grace later discovers the falsehood when she comes on Suke crunching nuts between her (flawless) jaws, like some human nutcracker. The speed and plausibility with which he comes up with his cover story implies that Fitzpiers has talked himself out of this kind of fix before.

3/16 *What precipitates Fitzpiers's professional decline, after marriage?* His impetuous resignation as the doctor in attendance at the local Union, or workhouse, on being reprimanded. His adversary Dr Jones meanwhile gains ground against him.

3/17 *What is the first occasion after marriage that Fitzpiers leaves home without a farewell kiss to Grace?* When he first goes off to treat Mrs Charmond, after she has been tipped out of her carriage (with the less than immense damage of a scratched forearm).

3/18 *Why does Suke consistently mis-address Grace as 'Miss Melbury'?* Because Suke regards herself as Fitzpiers's true mate—after their Midsummer tryst and subsequent affair. Does he, one wonders, continue to 'see' Suke after marriage?

3/19 *What, when an exhausted Darling brings an even more exhausted (and sleeping) Fitzpiers back to Hintock (after a clandestine visit to Felice at Middleton Abbey), are the first words that he says to his anxious wife?* 'Ah Felice . . . Oh—it's Grace.' The rat.

3/20 *Giles has a 'serious illness' during the winter, before the breakdown of the Fitzpiers marriage. What was the illness?* A variety of typhoid fever, as Fitzpiers later diagnoses it. The disease eventually returns to kill him.

3/21 *What spurious reason does Fitzpiers give for abandoning Grace, in the parting letter he sends her?* 'The animosity shown towards me by your father'.

3/22 *How, in his few intimate moments with her (and harking back, presumably, to their childhood years), does Giles Winterborne address the woman he has previously called 'Mrs Fitzpiers'?* 'Gracie'. Symbolically, it separates her from her married partner.

3/23 *Where is Felice buried, and where is Giles buried; and who faithfully attends their graves?* Felice Charmond is buried in Germany, Giles in Hintock graveyard. His grave is visited faithfully by Grace and Marty until the reconciliation with Fitzpiers, after which only Marty keeps her lover's vigil—until she too joins him under the Wessex soil, we guess. There is no intimation that she will ever love again. Felice's grave is unvisited.

3/24 *What does the vengeful Tim Tangs catch in the man-trap that he lays for Fitzpiers?* Grace's dress (women's dresses, of course, usually entrap men). Tim goes to New Zealand convinced he has paid out Fitzpiers by crippling him. Doubtless it cheers his voyage and the hard pioneering years that lie ahead for him and Suke.

3/25 *What is Marty's final epitaph on Giles?* 'You was a good man, and did good things!' Ungrammatical and monosyllabic as they are, her words are the most potent in the novel. Who, after Giles's death, will do good things in the woodland?

Level Four

4/1 *In his Preface, Hardy claims that 'the question of matrimonial divergence' (i.e. divorce) 'is left where it stood'. Although not what the Victorians called a 'social problem novel', does* The Woodlanders *hint at any Hardyan solution?* There is only one happy marriage that can be seen in the forefront of the narrative: that between the relatively ancient Melbury (sixty years old and more) and his second wife. His first marriage was, evidently, blighted by the 'trick' he played on Giles's father. Conceivably, a union between Giles and Grace might have been happy—if so it would be unusual in Hintock or, Hardy implies, anywhere else on God's (or godless) earth. The implication of the novel is that marriage is typically unhappy, and where the burden of unhappiness is intolerable, some civilized terminus should be allowed. This conclusion is, of course, even more strongly asserted in *Jude the Obscure*.

4/2 *Is Marty South a waif, or what the late Victorians called 'a new woman'?* Marty, so prominent in the opening chapters, and magnificently lamenting on the last page, can be seen, from one angle, as the perpetually victimized woman. But Hardy infuses her with some interesting social-historical significance. When we first see her, she is garbed as a man, 'With a bill-hook in one hand, and a leather glove much too large for her on the other . . . She wore a leather apron . . . which was much too large for her.' Her name could be applied to a young man as well as a young woman (i.e. short for 'Martin' as readily as 'Martha'). She is doing a man's job—more significantly, a skilled man's job—making wooden spars at eighteenpence a thousand. When he discovers what she is doing, Giles says, in amazement, 'But how could you learn to do it? 'Tis a trade'—with the implication that no mere woman could master a man's business in this way. Marty replies: 'Trade! . . . I'd be bound to learn it in two hours.' Elsewhere (barking trees, for example), Marty shows herself the equal, if not the superior, of her male co-workers. Her cropped head (like an apple on a gatepost, as Giles unkindly puts it) and the lack of 'womanly contours' (i.e. bosom) that the narrator observes, repeatedly suggest that Marty is as much a new woman as Sue Bridehead—with the difference that Marty's feminism is constructed around peasant hardiness rather than intellectualism and superfine sensibility.

4/3 *Is Mrs Charmond a good Lady of the Manor?* She has only a life interest in her great house and large properties, has no family connection with Hintock, and no circle of friends or acquaintance in the area. She evidently attends church, but why she comes to the village at all is not explained (it may, of course, have been a clause in her husband's will that she spend a certain portion of the year at Hintock). An actress in former life, she evidently prefers a bohemian style of life. And yet, as is noticed by the locals, her lack of interest is, in its way, passively benign. She rarely interferes or lords it over the community of which she is the titular head.

4/4 *Why did Melbury send his daughter off to distant boarding school (where she remains, apparently, even during school holidays)?* Mainly, as he repeatedly says, that she might better herself and rise above her father's low station in life—decontaminate herself, that is, from everything redolent of Wessex. It is clear that Grace is a bookish and intelligent girl and benefits from the education her father imposes on her. In her bedroom, her father lovingly preserves the brown spot above her bedside table, 'where her candle had been accustomed to stand, when she had used to read in bed till the midnight hour'. Other residents of Hintock turn in early in the evening lest, as Tim Tangs puts it, their faces be 'as long as clock-cases' next day. Grace is one of the admirable self-improving young women in Hardy's fiction, like Elizabeth-Jane Newson.

4/5 *What do we know of Mrs Charmond's late husband?* Only the basic facts that he was rich, old, and an ironmaster, and that he had a connoisseur's interest in 'man-traps and spring-guns and such articles', collecting them and relishing the histories of maiming, torture, and wounding they brought with them. Mr

Charmond himself, of course, fell into a man-trap of sorts, as Mrs Charmond archly observes to Grace. She is no trophy wife.

4/6 *What, if anything, indicates a certain sexual laxity in the lines of Fitzpiers's features?* 'The classical curve of his mouth was not without a looseness in its close.' Loose indeed.

4/7 *What are the two things we know Marty to write in the course of the novel?* The first is the chalk inscription, after John South's death, on the front of Giles's house: 'O Giles, you've lost your dwelling-place | And therefore, Giles, you'll lose your Grace' (which Grace later changes to 'keep your Grace'). The second is the letter to Fitzpiers, alerting him to the fact that Mrs Charmond's hair is, substantially, Marty's shorn locks—the fine lady's fine feathers are borrowed.

4/8 *Three women, as Fitzpiers watches, pass through the newly painted swing-gate by his front door. How different are their actions, and reactions?* Suke Damson, with 'skirts tucked up', dashes through, finds herself stained with the white paint (symbolically enough), swears and rubs herself in the grass (Fitzpiers laughs). Marty South, still wearing black for her father's death, merely looks at the stain, and stoically wipes it off 'with an unmoved face' (she is the longest-suffering character in the novel). When Grace comes, with her white boa and white gloves, she looks at the gate, and pushes it open with a stick, 'without touching it at all'. She is the most delicate (and efficient) of the three.

4/9 *What are the implications of Fitzpiers's affection for the poetry of Shelley?* It ties in with his love of the 'ideal'—but the poet's notorious sexual delinquency and his and Byron's 'league of incest' (a scandal only a few decades in the past at the time of the novel) suggest recklessness in affairs of the heart and a disregard for marriage law. Fitzpiers is unique in Hardy's fiction in being both a fornicator, an adulterer, and (finally, we hope) a faithful husband—until, as is cynically prophesied, another Suke Damson comes along.

4/10 *Why will Fitzpiers not rise in the 'profession he had chosen',* *even if (as his saving Grace from typhoid indicates) he is a skilled* *medical practitioner by the standards of his time?* He is 'a man of too many hobbies'. At the period in which he falls in love with Grace, and enjoys more carnal pleasures with Suke, his hobby is 'abstract philosophy'. Not a helpful source of knowledge for the ambitious medical man.

4/11 *How does Grace find Fitzpiers when she calls on him to plead* *for Grammer Oliver's brain?* Asleep in his living room, under his sofa hood, 'like a recumbent figure within some canopied mural tomb of the fifteenth century'. We are reminded of his connections with earls and the grand monument to his decayed family in Sherton-Abbas. It is, surprisingly, given the littleness of the Hintock world, Grace's first sight of the glamorous doctor (what physician, one wonders, does Melbury employ?).

4/12 *'Never could I deceive you,' protests Fitzpiers, 'fervently', on* *his first meeting with Grace. The narrator observes: 'Foreknowledge* *to the distance of a year or so, in either of them, might have spoilt the* *effect of that pretty speech.' Why does Hardy give his narrative game* *away in this way?* Such authorial predictions, over the head of the narrative to the reader, Henry James labelled 'suicidal'. But Hardy, one presumes, is willing to sacrifice suspense in the interest of creating a sense of juggernaut-like inevitability. A cloud of gloom hangs over Grace henceforth.

4/13 *Watching Fitzpiers make his addresses to Grace, and the simul-* *taneous accidental falling of two nesting 'love birds' (pheasants, pre-* *sumably) into the bonfire beneath, what does the rural philosopher* *Marty say?* 'That's the end of what is called love!' The birds part, going their separate ways, leaving a singed smell behind them. 'Nesting' may be a euphemism for 'copulating'.

4/14 *Mrs Charmond's discarded lover explains to Giles that he is 'an* *Italianized American, a South Carolinian by birth ... I left my* *native country on the failure of the Southern cause, and have never*

*returned to it since.' Is this statement something the novel otherwise
generally lacks, a precise dating reference?* On the face of it, yes. It
would seem that the American exile left in 1866, after the Civil
War, and joined the struggle for freedom in emergent Italy. This
would explain, among other things, his handiness with firearms.
But if the law which so excites Melbury later in the action is
the 1857 Matrimonial Causes (i.e. divorce) Act—which it surely
must be—there would seem to be a double time scheme at work
in the novel.

4/15 *What do we know of Fitzpiers's background?* Tantalizingly
little. As Melbury tells Grace, encouraging her to accept his offer
of marriage, on his mother's side Fitzpiers is connected with the
Lords Baxby of Sherton. But they are a great family no longer
and Baxby Castle is a ruin. Edred studied at Heidelberg, where he
had his brief love affair with Mrs Charmond. Whether he studied
at one of the British universities, or apprenticed himself to an
older doctor, we do not know. He has no blood relative that we
meet or hear of in the novel. No relative, apparently, comes to his
wedding. The reader assumes he bought his practice in Hintock—
which would have cost much less than an equivalent practice in
Budmouth (for which, later, he intends to borrow from his father-
in-law). It is not clear that he has private means—although he has
expensive tastes.

4/16 *What do we know of Mrs Charmond's background?* Fitzpiers
first came across her when he was studying in Heidelberg. She
was with her family there. At that time, she wore a 'long tail of
rare-coloured hair'. They talked, having met each other by chance
while out promenading. She dropped a handkerchief, he (following the codes of flirtation) picked it up, noticed the name
embroidered on it (Felice), and fell in love. Felice's mother, however, noticed the 'impecunious student' and, 'knowing my face
was my only fortune', bundled her daughter off to Baden. Thereafter, it seems, Felice may have gone on the stage (not, one assumes,
under her own name). In Italy, she evidently had an affair with
the American who eventually kills her. She subsequently married

Mr Charmond, the ironmaster from the north and the new owner of the Manor House at Hintock. He promptly died, leaving her a rich and eligibly young widow. We meet none of her relatives. She has packed much into her twenty-seven years—or, as she calls it, 'my battle with life'. Her proposed trip to the Mediterranean is, presumably, intended as something of a second husband-hunt.

4/17 *What, by way of refreshment, does Mrs Charmond offer Fitzpiers when he comes to attend on her for the first time?* A cigarette. She too is smoking one. They became fashionable after being brought back by British troops from the Crimea, but Mrs Charmond probably picked the habit up on the Continent. The redolence of cigarette smoke throws an erotic aroma over the scene.

4/18 *What reason does Fitzpiers give for taking up horse-riding (on the docile grey mare, Darling) and what is his real reason?* The ostensible reason is to get to his patients more efficiently. The real reason is to make clandestine calls on Felice, avoiding highway witnesses. Possibly, too, he may wish to avoid paying highway tolls.

4/19 *Does Winterborne ever do anything to or with Grace that could be thought to fall below the high standards of sexual morality he sets himself?* Only once, when, 'somnambulistically', he absent-mindedly caresses a flower on Grace's bosom and—one assumes—unintentionally caresses the breast beneath.

4/20 *When the two women are lost, like babes in the wood and, despite their rivalry, huddle together for warmth, Felice whispers a few words in Grace's ear which produce a convulsive effect. 'He's had you!' exclaims Grace. 'Can it be—can it be!' What are the 'few words'?* On the face of it, 'we have become lovers in the full sense of the word'. But there seems more implied than this. Grace knows of her husband's misconduct and must surely suspect that, over the last eight months more than flirting has occurred. Nor does she react as violently to the discovery of the Suke Damson involvement. Felice goes on to say, 'I am his slave'—hinting, perhaps, at some exotic sexual connection between the two of them, something more, surely, than mere adulterous liaison. Alternatively, Hardy could be seen to be invoking the Victorian truism that a woman becomes sexually helpless when in the power of her seducer. But, in the Fitzpiers–Charmond affair, who seduces whom?

4/21 *Is there any occasion on which the three women we know Fitzpiers has slept with during the novel come together?* Yes. When Fitzpiers, assaulted by his vengeful father-in-law, is reported to be dead or seriously injured, Suke and Mrs Charmond arrive at the Melbury home. It is not clear where they have heard the news of Fitzpiers's accident. Realizing the irony of the situation, Grace conducts her two sisters-in-intimacy into Fitzpiers's bedroom with the words: 'Wives all, let's enter together!' He is not, of course, in the bedroom. Later, he will stagger his bloody way to the Manor House, which leads to his subsequent scandalous open liaison with Mrs Charmond—the winner, for the moment, of the three-part competition for ownership of the glamorous doctor.

4/22 *Who are the only patients we know Fitzpiers has cured in his medical career?* Himself, by making a tourniquet with some halfpence and his handkerchief to stop the fatal bleeding after Melbury has hurled him (or let him fall) to the ground. And Grace, who is saved from typhoid by his mysterious brown medicine, brought back from Italy. His medical attentions kill John South and are unnecessary for Mrs Charmond's scratched arm.

4/23 *What is the only housework, so to call it, that we witness Felice Charmond performing?* At Fitzpiers's request, she washes his blood off the white-painted garden fence, which would betray his being in the house. 'What will not women do on such devoted occasions?' asks the narrative, sarcastically. If we are thinking of Felice Charmond, they will even take a washcloth in their manicured hands.

4/24 *When a shattered Melbury returns from London, with the news that, after all, 'unmarrying' is not simple, he explains, bitterly: 'He* *has not done you* enough *harm.' What does he mean?* Under the double standard of the 1857 Act, a wife's adultery sufficed for divorce, but a husband's adultery only if compounded with cruelty, unnatural practices, or other exacerbating factors.

4/25 *How does the Fitzpiers–Charmond liaison end?* Vaguely, we gather that Fitzpiers finally read Marty's letter, precipitating a separation from his lover. On her part, Felice 'repented' and left for Switzerland by herself. Evidently she subsequently returned to Germany. There she was tracked down and shot by her demented American admirer.

Tess of the d'Urbervilles

Level One

1/1 *Who informs Jack Durbeyfield about his noble pedigree?*
The Revd Tringham, a country vicar who is also an amateur
antiquarian and local historian.

1/2 *Who, as best the reader can piece together, are the Durbeyfield
children and what are their ages?* Abraham is nine at the beginning
of the narrative. He is the last male of the d'Urberville line
and the oldest boy in the family. The other Durbeyfield children,
as the action opens, are: Tess (something over sixteen), Liza-Lu
(something over twelve), Hope (age unknown, but plausibly
around seven), Modesty (five?), a three-year-old boy (unnamed),
and a one-year-old baby. The early scenes in the novel should be
played out in the reader's mind against a background of ceaseless
domestic clatter in the cramped Durbeyfield household. Given
Tess's age, the Durbeyfield parents can only have been married
some seventeen years and must be comparatively young (in their
late thirties or early forties) although the modern imagination
may tend to picture them as much older.

1/3 *Where is the d'Urberville family vault, and what does the place-
name mean?* Kingsbere (i.e. Bere Regis), the royal burial place. As
the (true) d'Urberville line peters out, in genetic exhaustion, the
narrative drifts towards this final resting place for its climactic
action.

1/4 *What is the name of the Durbeyfield horse and how old is he?*
Prince. We do not know the precise count of years but since, one
assumes, he was loyally named after the birth of Queen Victoria's
first male child (by Prince Albert) in 1842, one assumes the beast
is well into his twenties and should, were there any justice for
horses, be out at pasture.

1/5 *Is the carcass of Prince dispatched to the knacker's yard?* No. He is buried, with due ceremony, in the Durbeyfield garden. Despite the cash value of the dead animal 'Sir John' disdains to sell his Rosinante for cat's meat. Mrs Durbeyfield probably has a more practical view on things but is firmly under her lord and master's thumb.

1/6 *Where do the Stoke-d'Urbervilles live?* At the 'Chase'—they are by nature a predatory crew. The Chase, we are told, is 'one of the few remaining woodlands in England of undoubted primaeval date', associated with 'the hunt of the White Hart', whose symbolism is perhaps too obvious.

1/7 *Where does the Stoke-d'Urberville money come from?* Money-lending 'in the North', a business in which the family founder, Simon Stoke, made his fortune. 'Stoke' has associations of the northern town of that name and the steam power on which the Industrial Revolution was based. 'Simony' is a medieval term for 'usury'. Hardy is deft in what Henry James called 'the science of names'.

1/8 *When we first meet him, Alec is smoking. What?* A 'Havana', as we later learn. The cigar, it needs no Freud to tell us, is phallic, and stereotypical for the Victorian seducer on the prowl.

1/9 *How does Alec, squire that he is, first address Tess?* 'Well, my beauty'. The line, with its seigneurial overtones, comes straight from Victorian melodrama. This, one deduces, will not be the first pure maiden Alec has ruined.

1/10 *Is Alec, as the reader first encounters him, bearded?* No. He has a moustache, with 'curled points' which we may imagine him twirling lustfully when he espies some young female victim. Later in the narrative, after he experiences his religious rebirth, his gorgeous moustache is cut off.

1/11 *What variety of strawberry does Alec intrude, suggestively,* *into Tess's mouth?* 'British Queen'. It is an oddly disturbing detail.

1/12 *What is the 'abiding defect' of Trantridge?* It drinks hard.

1/13 *What does it mean when a cow goes 'azew'?* The animal's milk dries up. There is, as is common with Hardy's dialect usages, no concise way of saying it in standard English.

1/14 *What instrument does Angel play, and where did he get it?* A harp, inevitably (would angels play saxophones, or ukeleles?). The instrument is second-hand and was bought at a sale.

1/15 *Which three girls does Tess share her bedchamber with and what do we know about them?* Retty Priddle (the last of the Norman Paridelles, as Tess is the last of the d'Urbervilles), Izz Huett (Isabella, forever in love), and 'jolly faced' Marian.

1/16 *How far does the gallant Angel have to carry the girls across the flooded lane, on their way to church?* Fifty yards; far enough for an intimate warmth to develop. Hardy is ingenious in creating situations in which, despite the stern prohibitions of the time, unmarried young people can have (legitimate) physical contact (see, for example, the scene in *A Pair of Blue Eyes* in which the heroine tears off her petticoat to make a rope with which to save her lover, perilously hanging as he is on a sheer cliff).

1/17 *Where was Tess Durbeyfield born?* Marlott. Her lot in life is to be marred, the name suggests.

1/18 *What had Tess 'hoped to be'?* A teacher. Judging by the high opinion which her schoolteachers had of her (keeping her with them till she was fifteen) and her little instructional conversations with Abraham, Tess would have made an excellent teacher had fate been kinder to her.

1/19 *What happens to the confessional letter Tess sends Angel?* It slips under the carpet and is lost. She, poor woman, assumes he has read it and tactfully forbears to mention it. It is, perhaps, slightly odd that she should choose this cumbersome way of communicating her past to Angel—he discloses his 'impure' past verbally. 'Letters' (as in *Jude the Obscure*, where the 'letter killeth', or in *Far from the Madding Crowd*, where Bathsheba's valentine to Boldwood leads to murder and madness) can often be deadly in Hardy's fiction. Good things do not come in envelopes.

1/20 *Where does Angel resolve to go, after the separation?* To Brazil, on an emigration scheme (with assisted passage). A typically romantic gesture.

1/21 *Whom is Tess reunited with at Flintcomb-Ash, working in the fields?* Car Darch and her fair sister. Hardy seems to be making the point that it is a whole class of young women (irrespective of their very different personal characteristics), not just his tragic heroine, who are being exploited and ground down by the new agricultural practices of the later nineteenth century.

1/22 *How long must Tess, effectively an indentured serf, work for Farmer Groby?* Till Lady Day—6 April. She actually leaves before that date when Liza-Lu informs her that their mother 'is took very bad, and the doctor says she's dying'. By breaking her contract she will, presumably, have forfeited her terminal payment and Groby will have had her labour free of charge.

1/23 *Who dies first, Jack or Joan Durbeyfield?* He does, suddenly but not entirely unexpectedly, of fatty degeneration of the heart.

1/24 *Where does Tess 'give herself' to Alec, as opposed to being 'taken' by him, sexually?* Sandbourne (i.e. Bournemouth), a garish resort town, appropriate for the squalid event, the lowest point of the heroine's degradation.

1/25 *Whom does Mercy Chant finally marry?* Cuthbert Clare, it being the late 1860s when Oxford dons were finally permitted to marry.

Level Two

2/1 *Tess of the d'Urbervilles is a novel named after its heroine. What other names is the 'pure woman' known by in the narrative?* We are never quite sure if 'Tess' is short for 'Teresa' (a famously suffering saint—also connected with that other suffering heroine, Dorothea Brooke, in George Eliot's *Middlemarch*). Strictly speaking, Hardy's novel might have been entitled 'Tess Durbeyfield'—which would not, perhaps, have caught the purchaser's eye—or 'Tess Urberville' (the 'd' is redundant). Tess is addressed by her siblings (but never by her lovers) as 'Sissy'. Angel, during their lovemaking, uses the tender diminutive 'Tessy'. She is, for the second part of the narrative, 'Tess Clare'—although the name sounds strange to the reader's ear. When registered in The Herons, Tess goes under the name of 'Mrs d'Urberville', which, of course, she is not.

2/2 *The reader first encounters Tess in May, walking with her 'club'. She carries a 'peeled willow-wand'. What does it signify?* At the Roman festival of Lupercal, the wand bestowed fertility. It is the same rite introduced in the opening scenes of Shakespeare's *Julius Caesar* where Caesar asks his young friend to touch the barren Calphurnia with the Lupercalian wand. It prophesies the unlucky fecundity that will doom Tess's chances in life—and bring her, in two senses, 'Sorrow'.

2/3 *How old is Tess and what does her age signify?* We are not told directly how old Tess is but we do know that she is four years older than Liza-Lu, which would make her around sixteen and a half. At the time Hardy was writing, this would have been a few months over the newly imposed 'age of consent' for women. A legally virginal target for predators on the prowl like Alec.

2/4 *How far is the Vale of Blackmoor from London?* Four hours distant (and a whole world away). Hardy is, presumably, thinking of the train link opened from Dorchester to the metropolis in the late 1840s. Hardy distinguishes carefully between those parts of Wessex the railway has reached and those it has merely 'engirdled', such as the Vale of Froome and Flintcomb-Ash.

2/5 *When did Tess leave the village school?* 'A year or two before this date', i.e. when she was around fifteen years old. This would be, by the standards of the time, a protracted education for a working-class girl. Young Tess, we are told, had a 'leading' place in the school and helped out the teachers. She is obviously bright and more literate than her fellow dairymaids at Farmer Crick's.

2/6 *What are the crest and arms of the Stoke-d'Urbervilles?* A castle, lion rampant; heraldically symbolic of money and rapacity.

2/7 *When he first meets Tess, Alec, the cad, is fascinated by one particular aspect of her physical appearance. What is it?* The 'luxuriance' of her figure—her breasts, that is.

2/8 *When Alec comes calling to see if she will accept employment with his ('their') family, where does Tess go to think it over?* Among the gooseberry bushes—shrubs which have associations with the babies proverbially found under them. An ill omen. It is the iller omen since Prince is buried there.

2/9 *What, according to Joan Durbeyfield, is Tess's 'trump card'?* 'Her face—as 'twas mine.' She may be fibbing—it is Tess's 'luxuriant' body which may be her trump card. For Angel, of course, her trump card (something that Joan could never imagine) is her genetic 'purity'. An illusory purity, as it transpires.

2/10 *What is Tess employed to do by the d'Urbervilles?* She works as their poultry keeper. Specifically, she cares for their alien (non-Wessex) and exotic breeds of bird: Hamburghs, Cochins, Brahmas, Dorkings, etc. New kinds of animal husbandry, we gather, are replacing those traditional in the region. No humble roosters for the d'Urbervilles.

2/11 *What colour are Tess's eyes?* Neither black, nor blue, nor gray, nor violet 'but all those shades together'. It is not a hue which one can easily imagine.

2/12 *What is 'Dairyman Dick' called on Sundays?* 'Mister Richard Crick.'

2/13 *What is Angel's ambition in life, during his stay at Talbothays?* To farm in the colonies, in America, or at home. He apparently has no preference (knowing, one suspects, little about the different kinds of agriculture involved). There is no indication that Angel will be a particularly expert farmer nor that, at the end of the novel, tilling the earth will be his ultimate vocation in life. 'Farming', like other features of his behaviour, seems the manifestation of an unworldly idealism ('a return to the soil').

2/14 *What gives Dairyman Crick's butter a 'twang'?* The garlic which, unluckily, his dairy cows ingest. A posse is mustered to discover and root out the dangerous bulbs.

2/15 *Whom was Marian, Tess's comrade, going to marry, before she fell hopelessly in love with Angel?* 'A dairyman at Stickleford' who had twice asked her.

2/16 *Whom do Angel's parents intend their son to marry?* Mercy Chant, a girl of his own class and background.

2/17 *What ominous event commemorates the marriage of Tess and Angel?* The afternoon crowing of a cock.

2/18 *What quotation (mangled) from Browning passes through Angel's mind as he and Tess part?* 'God's *not* in his heaven'—a reversal of the pious girl's refrain ('God's in his heaven | All's right with the world') in the poem *Pippa Passes*.

2/19 *Whom does Angel ask to accompany him to Brazil?* Izz Huett. He later withdraws the invitation after she, loyal to her friend, tells him that Tess 'would have laid down her life for 'ee'. The invitation—with its implied reflection of Angel's thinking ('one dairymaid is as good as another') does not speak well for the young man, any more than does his taking up with Liza-Lu ('one Durbeyfield is as good as another') at the end of the novel.

2/20 *What does Marian call Flintcomb-Ash?* 'A starve-acre place'—that is, the soil is thin, poor, and good for nothing.

2/21 *How does Tess celebrate her first wedding anniversary?* She dresses up to visit her in-laws. In the event, she does not go, fearing humiliation.

2/22 *What happens to Tess's boots, when she makes her abortive visit to her in-laws?* Having done most of the journey in them (to protect her best footwear) she takes them off by the side of the road and leaves them to be collected later. They are subsequently picked up by Cuthbert and given away. Tess has to walk home in the patent leather shoes she had hoped to protect.

2/23 *What work does Tess first do in the fields, having taken responsibility for supporting her family?* Hacking swedes—that is, rooting the vegetables out of the soil. Muddy, hard, stooping labour. Swedes would be cattle food, principally.

2/24 *What is the form of Alec's proposal to Tess?* That she marry him and accompany him on his proposed work as a missionary in Africa. She becomes his mistress instead.

2/25 *Where do Angel and Tess finally consummate their marriage?* Bramshurst Court, over the course of their five-day furtive sojourn in the place. It is one of the more delayed honeymoons in Victorian fiction. Afterwards, of course, it would have been impossible for Angel to have divorced Tess since he would have been judged to have condoned her infidelities.

Level Three

3/1 *How is Jack, Tess's father, related to the d'Urberville line if that line (originating with the Norman invaders) is, as we are told, 'extinct' and the name no longer current in the almanacs of British nobility?* Jack's great-grandfather, we are told (darkly), 'had secrets, and didn't care to talk of where he come from'. He suffered, we assume, from the stigma of bastardy—a painful affliction in the nineteenth century. There were, it would seem, no legitimate male heirs to the d'Urberville title. As an illegitimate offspring (if that was what he was), Jack's father should, by law, have taken his mother's surname—but evidently he assumed the slightly debased 'Durbeyfield'—sufficient of a clue for the Revd Tringham to identify the last of the true d'Urberville stock.

3/2 *Name the three Clare brothers in order of age. What are they doing when we first encounter them? Are there other Clare siblings?* The brothers are, in order of age: Felix, Cuthbert, Angel. Felix, when we first encounter the trio, is a curate; Cuthbert is still an undergraduate, destined for an academic, or clerical career; Angel is uncommitted, uncertain of his beliefs, and drifting towards freethinking. When we first encounter them the brothers have embarked on a 'reading party'—rural excursions popularized at Oxford in the 1840s, in which young men from the university would go off into the country. There they would read and discuss select texts. The Clare brothers are hacking away at *A Counterblast to Agnosticism* (the incendiary term recently introduced into intellectual discourse by T. H. Huxley). There is a half-sister in the family whom we never meet. The family background (against which Angel is half-inclined to rebel) is solidly Anglican, with a strong evangelical flavour.

3/3 *Does Tess take after her mother or her father?* In regard to her frontal development (her full breasts), her mother. She also has her mother's skills as a dairymaid (acquired rather than inherited, one assumes). Nonetheless, through her father (deficient as he signally is in them) she has inherited the aristocratic 'fineness' of the d'Urbervilles. Tess is a rustic aristocrat.

3/4 *How does Prince die, and why does the tragedy happen?* A drowsy Tess, driving at night, falls asleep at the reins and her cart veers to the wrong side of the road. The mail coach, with its rubberized 'noiseless wheels' and right of way, crashes into Prince. The buried metaphor in the horse's name is revived by the description of the death blow: 'The pointed shaft of the cart had entered the breast of the unhappy Prince like a sword.' Since the death of Albert, the tragic death of princes had resonance in late-Victorian England.

3/5 *When and how did Tess pick up her dairymaid skills?* She learned them 'when her father had owned cows' (drink, one assumes, explains his decline to the status of humble haggler). Before her marriage to Jack Durbeyfield Tess's mother had been a dairymaid.

3/6 *How does Tess arrive at Trantridge to work?* She walks alongside Alec's gig, after he has terrorized her into giving him a kiss. The awkwardness (he driving, she nervously in tow) suggests the future complications of their relationship.

3/7 *Where does Mrs d'Urberville keep her bullfinches?* The birds are permitted to fly loose in her bedroom, where, as they defecate, they leave 'white spots' on the furnishings. One of Tess's jobs is to whistle to the birds and, presumably, clean up after them.

3/8 *What is 'scroff' and what part does it play in Tess's downfall?* Scroff is dust which, during the dance, rises and gets under skirts, and soils the sweating dancers. This is the prelude to Tess's calamitous surrender to Alec in The Chase. Details such as this indicate how hard this novelist pressed against the censorious standards of 'decency' in Victorian fiction. As he says elsewhere, Hardy is writing for readers of 'full age'.

3/9 *Who is Car Darch and what is her nickname?* Miss Darch is a late, and discarded, favourite (i.e. mistress) of Alec's. Her nickname is 'Queen of Spades'—(as in Pushkin's short story, the death card). Her fair-haired sister, Nancy, nicknamed the 'Queen of Diamonds', has also previously been Alec's mistress. Tess, sadly, will make up the trio.

3/10 *How long does Tess stay at Trantridge before returning home, 'a maiden no more'?* Four months, June to October, the traditional harvesting season. She too has been (in Shakespearian parlance) 'cropped'.

3/11 *What is the name of Tess's child, and who christens the babe?* Sorrow (the Undesired) is the unfortunate infant's name. She christens him herself.

3/12 *What urn does Tess raise over her child's grave?* A Keelwell (i.e. Keiller's) marmalade jar. The processed product would have been a relatively late arrival in Wessex, displacing traditional honey, apple jelly, and plum jam.

3/13 *What are the names of Tess's favourite eight cows among the ninety-five in the Crick herd? Which is she milking when Angel 'almost' kisses her and says he loves her? How does the cow react?* Tess's favourites are: Dumpling, Fancy, Lofty, Mist, Old Pretty, Young Pretty, Tidy, and Loud. She is milking Old Pretty when Angel makes his surprising advance to her. Old Pretty (too old for such nonsense apparently) is unamused, and threatens to kick over the milking pail.

3/14 *What present does Mrs Crick send Mrs Clare, Angel's mother, the clergyman's wife, and what does Mrs Clare do with it?* Black pudding (i.e. cooked offal sausage) and mead (fermented honey drink). The vicar's wife gives the food to a man with delirium tremens and prudently puts the drink in the medicine cabinet.

3/15 *What text was it on which the Revd Clare (Angel's father)* preached (in the distant past) which so annoyed young Alec? 'Thou fool, this night thy soul shall be required of thee.' Eventually the vicar's words take root in the sinner's heart, impelling him towards (shortlived) penitence and conversion.

3/16 *What happens to faithless Jack Dollop, a warning to other breakers of young girls' hearts?* He marries a widow woman with £50 a year, for which he is tossed in the butter-churn by the mother of the (penniless but loving) maid he jilted. Unhappily, no mother is on hand to do the same to Alec d'Urberville.

3/17 *Does Tess, under twenty-one, need permission to marry?* Strictly, she may do, if only to satisfy propriety. She seems not to demand it, judging by her mother's letter ('we . . . hear that you are going really to be married soon').

3/18 *When do Tess and Angel determine to marry?* They marry on New Year's Eve, by licence. Neither set of parents attends the service. Crick gives the bride away. We are not told precisely where they marry.

3/19 *Whence arises the d'Urberville 'curse', mentioned several times in the text?* From rape and murder, in their days of seigneurial authority (authority they abused), we deduce. When the Stoke-d'Urbervilles acquired (or bought) the family name, they evidently bought the curse along with it.

3/20 *How do Retty, Izz, and Marian react to the marriage of Angel and Tess?* Retty, the most desperate of the trio, tries to drown herself. Marian, more practical by nature, gets herself dead drunk by the willow bed (willows being proverbially associated with unhappy maidens). Marian is very low.

3/21 *When, on the 'honeymoon', Angel sleepwalks into Tess's bedroom, what does he say and what does it mean?* 'Dead, dead, dead' (echoing Lear's agonized valediction for Cordelia). What, however, does it mean? That the marriage is dead? That he wishes he were dead? That he wishes Tess were dead? 'Wretched, wretched, wretched' would be easier to make sense of. But deep in his unconscious, apparently, is a death wish. Tess, at the end of her unhappy life, will indeed hang at the end of a rope (like Cordelia again), dead, dead, dead.

3/22 *Does Tess know that Angel has gone to Brazil?* Apparently not. She keeps writing to him in England. Since he invited one of her closest friends to accompany him it is strange that word of his desperate act has not reached her.

3/23 *When, persecuted by rumour and gossip from Trantridge, Tess sleeps in the wood by Chalk-Newton, whom does she have for company?* A wounded pheasant. It is November, the shooting season. They are both of them victims of predatory males.

3/24 *What does the 'Cross-in-Hand' commemorate?* No one is quite sure. A stone pillar (which stands to this day) erected in a field, it may memorialize a murder, a miracle, or perhaps both. It is a wholly enigmatic monument. Later we are told of the legend that a murderer was once nailed by the hand there—as a kind of crucifixion. Tess's punishment is no less savage.

3/25 *What does Alec, after being born again a Christian, take up by way of occupation?* He becomes a 'ranter', or hellfire barn preacher. His diabolic whiskers are shaven off. Hardy gives tantalizingly few details as to how this amazing change of character occurred.

Level Four

4/1 *Hardy subtitled his novel 'A Pure Woman', in oblique antithesis to such section titles as 'Maiden' and 'Maiden No More'. What would have been the resonances of 'pure' to the late Victorian ear?* It is a complex question. There were, of course, moral 'purity campaigns', although the word also connoted the more practical campaigns against adulteration of food products. There are also overtones of the Max Nordau thesis (very popular in the 1890s) of 'Degeneration' and the inevitably increasing impurity of the English racial stock. Angel, it would seem, is—among all his other ideological affiliations—something of a eugenicist.

4/2 *What do we know of the d'Urbervilles and what, historically, does the name imply?* Inevitably the Frenchness of the name associates them with the 'Norman Yoke Thesis'—popularized in Scott's *Ivanhoe*. The NYT alleged that a primal and beautiful Saxon democracy had been extinguished by the brutal Norman invader in 1066 and only finally re-emerged in the nineteenth century. The d'Urbervilles decline as 'Norman blood unaided by Victorian lucre' (it is Alec's family's lucre which purchases the cursed name). The scraps of genealogical history we are given in the novel are by no means lustrous. They include the d'Urbervilles' participation in the bloody conquest of Glamorgan. The family enriched themselves during the reign of the usurper John (evil monarch of *Ivanhoe*). They 'declined a little in Oliver Cromwell's time'. On the Restoration, they were made 'Knights of the Royal Oak' (in commemoration of the fugitive King Charles's hiding place). They were, as we deduce from the ruminations on Tess's fate in The Chase, rapists, wastrels, and brutes. Their extinction is no great loss to the human race.

4/3 *What is Tess's mother singing when we first encounter her and what does the song signify?* 'The Spotted Cow'—the sad tale of a seduced ('spotted') milkmaid, who loses her maidenhood in a wood. It is a 'washing song'—ironic, since some 'stains' (such as the loss of maidenhood) are indelible, however hard the washerwoman scrubs. Tess's mother used to be a milkmaid, which makes one suspicious of the circumstances in which she married her husband, Jack. Tess, that is, may have been conceived out of wedlock.

4/4 *How well educated is Tess?* Reasonably well by any standard, and extremely well for a girl of her class, time, and region. She can write correct and grammatical letters (such as that to Angel which goes so sadly astray) and she can, when occasion requires, speak 'standard' English. Hardy is quite precise about the education Tess has received. She first attended a National School (institutions which preceded the 1870 Universal Education Act) and reached the sixth standard there. She had aspirations to be a school teacher, like her 'London trained' instructor at the school.

4/5 *What is the significance of the name 'Abraham', bestowed on the sickly eldest son and heir of the Durbeyfield family?* The patriarchal, dynasty-founding Christian name is an example of Hardy's irony. Abraham in the novel is the end of the d'Urberville line, not, like his Old Testament namesake, its progenitor.

4/6 *When he is sent to Rolliver's off-licence establishment to bring back his inebriated father, Abraham overhears the drunken boast that Tess will marry a rich d'Urberville relative 'and we'll ride in her coach, and wear black clothes'. Why black?* It is the 1860s. The villagers have all seen pictures of Queen Victoria making her appearance, in widow's weeds, as she makes her way (after her long mourning) to open Parliament, in her coach, in 1867. This would have struck a chord with *Graphic* readers of the serialized *Tess of the d'Urbervilles*.

4/7 *While they are carting the beehives to Casterbridge (a journey which will end in disaster and the death of Prince), Abraham asks Tess if the stars are 'worlds'. Yes, she replies. Some are splendid and some are 'blighted'. What has put this idea into Abraham's head and what prompts Tess's answer?* Bright schoolgirl that she is, Tess has picked up the current controversy initiated by William Whewell's *Of the Plurality of Worlds* (1853) which made rational arguments against there being more than one world in the universe. It was countered by Sir David Brewster's *More Worlds Than One* (1854) and Dionysus Lardner's *The Planets: Are They Inhabited Worlds?* (1854). Extra-terrestrial life was a burning topic of discussion in the late 1850s and 1860s (when *Tess of the d'Urbervilles* is set). Tess has evidently thought out her own views on the matter.

4/8 *What would be the contemporary resonance of the remark about Mrs d'Urberville that she 'was not the first mother to love her offspring resentfully, and to be bitterly fond'?* The contemporary reader might perhaps think of Queen Victoria and the errant and playboyish Prince of Wales.

4/9 *After Tess leaves Trantridge what does a distraught Alec do, and why?* He goes off to London—with fleshpots in mind—but apparently stops at Emminster, where he hears the Revd James Clare, Angel's father ('the last of the Old Low Church sort') preach. Alec is converted. His ostensible reason for leaving Trantridge is that he can't stand the 'old woman', his mother.

4/10 *Does Alec (who once said 'I'll never do anything against your will') 'rape' Tess?* Victorian commentators, in general, thought not. For them, Tess was 'seduced'—a moral but not a criminal offence on Alec's part. Modern commentators tend to conceive what happens in The Chase as rape. It remains ambiguous as Hardy chose to describe it. Alec, it will be remembered, 'rescues' Tess from the orgy at Chaseborough, scooping her up onto his horse. He deliberately loses his way, wandering off the Trantridge road in the wilderness of The Chase, 'the oldest wood in England'. Tess, who has been up since five every day that week, is exhausted and falls asleep in the saddle. She repulses some tentative lovemaking movements of Alec's, but seems to relent somewhat as they ride on. They lose themselves in the fog. Alec places her in a 'sort of couch or nest' made of dropped leaves and goes off to look for the path home. He finds it and returns to find Tess fast asleep. He bends down to her, 'till her breath warmed his face, and in a moment his cheek was in contact with hers. She was sleeping soundly, and upon her eyelashes there lingered tears.' This is the last image Hardy leaves us with. It could be Prince Charming about to wake Sleeping Beauty, or it could be ravishing Tarquin. The narrative averts its eyes from whatever happens next— seduction or rape. Readers can take their pick.

4/11 *Does Tess know for certain that she is pregnant when she and*

Alec part? It's not clear that she does, and it is made less clear by Hardy's time jump from 'sad October' to the following August. Tess's mother, of course, is currently pregnant with her seventh child. Had Tess known, and told Alec, he *might* perhaps have done the decent thing, atypical as it would have been.

4/12 *What may we assume about Angel's politics?* Since he believes, as we are told, in 'communistic' rule, one assumes he is a follower of William Morris and John Ruskin. He admires Whitman, and Whitmanesque 'comradeship' (something practised, elsewhere, by Jude and Sue). Angel is, we gather, 'agnostic'. This would debar him from attending university, like his more dutiful brothers. He rejects his father's 'evangelical school' of religion—although whether this has led to a violent filial rebellion (as, say, in Samuel Butler's *The Way of All Flesh*) is not clear. At the end of the novel, however, Angel is seen praying. Alec, it would seem, is not the only man to undergo religious conversion in the novel.

4/13 *Tess is milking when Angel first declares his love, and skimming milk in the churn when he proposes. What is she doing when she says she will, soon, give him an answer to his proposal? And what is she doing when she finally says yes, she will marry him?* Tess is making cheese when she says she will consider Angel's offer. She is delivering cans of milk to the station for transport to London on the early 'milk train' (so townspeople can have country fresh milk in their morning tea) when she finally agrees to marriage with Angel.

4/14 *What is Angel's wedding-night 'confession' to Tess?* That, several years before, during forty-eight hours of dissipation in London, he slept with a woman of the streets. The fact that it is well in the past reassures the reader (as, perhaps, it reassures Tess) that there is no legacy of disease from this lapse. One wonders whether it was before, or after, he and his brothers first caught a glimpse of Tess at her 'club', clad in white, willow-wand in hand, an incarnation of purity. Was Angel 'pure' as well?

4/15 *Tess tells Angel, 'you can get rid of me . . . By divorcing me'.*

Can he? Under the 1857 law, probably yes, on the grounds of her flagrant and provable misconduct with Alec. She, however, could not divorce him on the grounds of his equally provable desertion of her (to go off to Brazil) and his failure to support him. The 1857 Act was heavily biased in favour of husbands.

4/16 *Tess thinks of hanging herself with the cord of a box, on her disastrous wedding night. Why does she refrain?* Because 'I was afraid that it might cause a scandal to your [Angel's] name', now, of course, her name. It is, presumably, as Mrs Angel Clare that she is tried and hanged at Wintoncester, so even more scandal will, eventually, be brought on the family name.

4/17 *How much money does Angel give Tess on their parting, and what does she do with it?* He gives her £50 (the same sum that Jack Dollop married his widow for). She gives half the sum to her parents. It seems a one-off payment. Does Angel, one wonders, mean to support his wife—as, legally, he is obliged to? Or, dimly, does he intend to seek annulment of the union, on the grounds that the marriage was never consummated?

4/18 *What does Angel Clare, in his distress, whisper in the ear of Mercy Chant and what is her reaction?* 'The most heterodox ideas he could think of.' Mercy reacts with horror, and thereafter directs her affections to Cuthbert, now a dean at Cambridge. What this most heterodox idea can be ('There is no God'? 'Darwin is right'?) we are left to guess.

4/19 *How does Hardy describe the unnaturalness of the depopulation of the Wessex countryside and the drift of uprooted families like the Durbeyfields to towns, where destitution awaits them?* It is like 'the tendency of water to flow uphill when forced by machinery'. Hardy's social protest in novels like *Tess of the d'Urbervilles* is understated (compared, for example, to the ranting in fiction of writers like Charles Kingsley) but no less powerful for being understated. The Durbeyfields are not just one tragically unlucky family, but representatives of a whole victimized class.

4/20 *Why, as we eventually learn, did Alec never try to find out anything about Tess, after she left Trantridge? Why, for example, did he not trouble to enquire whether or not she was pregnant after their night in The Chase?* As he explains, it was because he went far away, to the north of England, shaking the dust of Wessex off his shoes. 'I knew nothing of this [the child] till now!' he protests. A serial seducer of women (for example, the Darch sisters), he must surely have been aware that pregnancy was a hazard for the women he ruined. Are there other bastards than Sorrow the Undesired? Plausibly, yes.

4/21 *Does Tess 'murder' Alec?* Victorian commentators, in general, thought so. Modern commentators are more forgiving of Tess's stabbing Alec. The principal evidence (since Hardy declines to describe the trial) comes from the landlady at The Herons, the lodging-house where Alec and Tess have taken an apartment. Mrs Brooks, an attentive proprietor of a 'decent' house, looks through the keyhole. It is morning. She sees Tess in distress at the breakfast-table and hears a long complaint ('a dirge rather than a soliloquy') from her lips. Tess, it seems, is berating herself for her weakness in surrendering again to Alec's 'cruel persuasions'. Mrs Brooks hears 'more and sharper words from the man' then a 'sudden rustle'. Tess leaves the house. Alec's body is subsequently discovered on the bed, stabbed through the heart. Later, to Angel, Tess explains, 'He heard me crying about you, and he bitterly taunted me; and called you by a foul name; and then I did it.' Did what? She evidently picked up the carving knife from the table, walked over to the bed, aimed the knife precisely at the dozing man, and—premeditatedly and cold-bloodedly—stabbed him through the heart. As a country girl who had worked on a farm, Tess would know all about slaughtering. Hardy, one presumes, does not narrate the trial because it would predispose the reader against the heroine, his 'pure woman', who—whatever the provocation—is surely as much a murderess as Bill Sikes.

4/22 *How do the police know that Mr and Mrs Angel Clare are at*

Stonehenge? The housekeeper at Bramshurst, we assume, must have snitched. Such ladies (as we recall from The Herons) are a sharp-eyed crew. The authorities dispatch no fewer than sixteen officers and a team of bloodhounds. It seems rather 'mob-handed' for the arrest of Tess of the d'Urbervilles.

4/23 *Angel, at the time of Tess's arrest at Stonehenge, kneels along-side Tess as she lies outstretched on the sacrificial altar. Is he perhaps praying?* Yes, presumably. But to which god? That cruel Jehovah of his father, or the druids' no less savage god(s)? Or, perhaps, the Greek tragedian's 'Immortals' invoked in the last lines of the novel?

4/24 *Is Tess pregnant at the time of her execution?* She may well be. The hanging is four months after her second 'honeymoon'. This is exactly the length of time it took her to discover that she was pregnant by Alec. A plea for delay should, surely, have been entered on her behalf in court. Did Angel, one wonders, secure the service of first-class lawyers for her defence? It seems that, hopeless idealist that he is, he may not have done. Trollope's Sergeant Chaffanbrass (or the unnamed lawyer who acts for Boldwood in *Far from the Madding Crowd*) could surely have saved Tess from the gallows until the child was born.

4/25 *At the end of the novel, Angel it seems will want to marry his deceased wife's sister, Liza-Lu. Can he?* Not in England, until a change in the law in 1905. He may, as he once wanted to, emigrate to South Africa, or America, where such marriages were permitted. Or he may simply flout the marriage laws.

Jude the Obscure

Level One

1/1 *Jude is eleven years old at the time of the novel's opening, as Phillotson takes his leave of Marygreen. The little boy has, we learn, only attended 'night school' with the village teacher. Why?* Before 1870 there was no obligation on children to attend school. Jude's 'self-help' (as Samuel Smiles famously called it) begins very early.

1/2 *What task is Jude engaged on when we first encounter him?* Drawing water from the village well. His other occupation, we learn, is as a rook-scarer for Farmer Troutham.

1/3 *What is the oldest, and what the newest, public structure in Marygreen?* The well is the oldest (soon, we hope, to be replaced by mains sanitation). The 'restored' Gothic church is, superficially at least, the newest. Hardy disapproved mightily of 'restoration', and wrote a novel attacking it (*The Laodiceans*)—his disapproval was the sharper for having himself, as a young mason, participated in such church 'improvement'.

1/4 *What did Jude's father die of?* The shakings—possibly 'ague', or malaria, more likely delirium tremens ('the shakes'). We only learn about Jude's background when Arabella spitefully enlightens him as to his father's domestic brutality and his mother's consequent suicide. 'The Fawleys were not made for wedlock', as his great-aunt says. Jude's thoroughgoing ignorance of his family background is one of the minor mysteries of the novel.

1/5 *How long has Jude been residing with his great-aunt Drusilla, as the novel opens?* A year. He has come to stay with her from south Wessex—some fifty miles, far away in the topography of Hardy's fiction.

1/6 *What is the picture on the wall of the inn where Jude takes Arabella on the first time they go walking, on Sunday?* Samson and Delilah.

1/7 *Where does Arabella go, after deserting Jude, and why?* She emigrates with her family to Australia. Pig-jobbing in Wessex is not profitable.

1/8 *What 'idols' does Sue buy, and what does she tell Miss Fontover they are?* Plaster casts of Venus and Apollo. She tells her unsuspecting landlady that the statuettes are of St Peter and Mary Magdalen.

1/9 *How does Jude raise the money to return to Marygreen?* He pawns his waistcoat. It is a good sign that he does not pawn his mason's tools.

1/10 *Where would Sue rather sit than in the cathedral?* The railway station. The cathedral has had its day, in her atheistic view of things.

1/11 *What musical instrument does Jude play?* The harmonium. He can also pick out a tune on the piano (presumably he practised on Phillotson's instrument). Hardy, on the evidence of *Under the Greenwood Tree*, disliked the newfangled harmonium. The instrument was invented in France in 1840, and became something of a fashion with religious families in the following decades.

1/12 *What wedding present does Jude give Sue?* A piece of white tulle, symbolizing purity.

1/13 *What is the 'turning-point in Jude's career'?* Sue's (Mrs Phillotson's) adulterous kiss, that induces him to burn his books as so much 'rubbidge'. It begins his long and tortuous descent into freethinking and Sue's even more tortuous ascent into religious exaltation—something that will utterly reverse their respective philosophies of life.

1/14 *What is it that gives Mr Phillotson earache?* The ventilator in his classroom. It reminds us of the reforms which have taken place in school architecture and layout. The school at Marygreen, we guess, had no such amenities. But reform (as with church restoration) is always two-edged and potentially 'headachy' in Hardy's world.

1/15 *Where did Gillingham and Phillotson go to school, and where to college?* Shaston, and Wintoncester Training College.

1/16 *What does Gillingham suggest is the best remedy for Sue, the errant wife of his best friend?* She should be 'smacked'. He is, presumably, that kind of schoolteacher. For some Victorians (those not influenced by the 'eccentric' doctrines of John Stuart Mill), this 'spare the rod and spoil the wife' would not seem necessarily brutal—if a trifle uncivilized.

1/17 *What is Phillotson's hobby?* The Roman antiquities of Wessex. He is an old man (in his habits if not in years), and obsessed with the ancients.

1/18 *Who is 'Age masquerading as Juvenility'?* Little Father Time—although, since Sue says to Jude 'I see you in him', it could conceivably be the young fellow's father, Jude.

1/19 *Why does Sue object so vehemently to the Register Office wedding which has been arranged?* It is, she complains, 'vulgar'. Her comment is either snobbish (Sue, as her exchanges with Arabella indicate, is uneasy when dealing with her 'inferiors') or an early indication of her incipient religious mania (only church weddings are 'real'). Jude feels no such inhibition.

1/20 *What 'failing' do Jude and Sue share and is it, in fact, a defect?* They are both horribly 'sensitive'. Is it a failing? The novel leaves the issue ambiguously poised.

1/21 *How much does Arabella pay Physician Vilbert for the love* *philtre, and what is it (allegedly) made from?* Five shillings—a huge amount, given, for example, that Phillotson's salary as a schoolteacher varies between £50 and £200 p.a. It is distilled, according to the physician, from nearly a hundred dove (i.e. pigeon) hearts.

1/22 *What was the scandal at Gaymead church?* The drunken masonry workers left the 'Nots' out of the carving of the Ten Commandments. A resurgence, we apprehend, of ancient Wessex paganism.

1/23 *Jude's first symptoms of the sickness which will eventually kill him show themselves at Aldbrickham. What is the sickness?* He later refers to it as 'inflammation of the lungs', and reference is made to having to work in the open air, in all seasons, and in windowless draughty buildings. It could be consumption, or bronchitis. But, given the huge amount of stone dust he must have inhaled, from the yards in which stone was cut up by saws and chisels, it seems quite likely that he had an 'industrial injury'—pneumoconiosis, or 'black lung'.

1/24 *What, as we learn late in the novel, was Jude's nickname among his workmates when he first came to Christminster?* 'Tutor of St Slums.'

1/25 *What ceremony is going on, noisily, as Jude dies?* The awarding of degrees.

Level Two

2/1 *Like many novelists, Hardy tried out a number of titles before coming up with the (lugubrious) Jude the Obscure. Among his trial titles were 'The Simpletons', 'Hearts Insurgent', and 'The Recalcitrants'. These are all plural, while the finally chosen title is singularly focused on the named hero (who was also, at one point, less felicitously named 'Jack'). Who, other than Jude, was simple,*

*recalcitrant, or the owner of an insurgent heart? Is anything the-
matic to be learned from this array of discards?* The titles, one
guesses, indicate uncertainty in Hardy's conception of his principal characters, rather than any clear distillation of issues.
There is, for example, a contradiction between being naive (or
'simple') and downright stubborn (or 'recalcitrant'). Are Jude
and Sue (and possibly Phillotson) innocents, or do they wilfully
kick against the pricks? Surely, too, Phillotson and Arabella are
not possessed of 'insurgent' (i.e. rebellious, or revolutionary)
hearts?

2/2 *Like 'former productions', Hardy insists,* Jude the Obscure *is
simply an endeavour to give shape and coherence to a series of seemings'. The usage 'seemings' is quaint. What does he have in mind?*
Like his friend the Dorset poet William Barnes, Hardy was
always keen to Anglicize his idiom. 'Seemings' renders into
English the currently fashionable French 'impressionism'. It also
implies a sceptical lack of certainty about the essential reality of
things that is habitual to this most sceptical of novelists.

2/3 *Aunt Drusilla's first remark to Jude (after some routine complaining) is: 'Jude my child, don't* you *ever marry. 'Tisn't for the
Fawleys to take that step any more.' Why not?* The Fawley–
Bridehead stock, she implies, has been weakened by intermarriage
and by moral degeneration.

2/4 *In which season of the year does the narrative begin?* 'Seed-
time'—the new year. Little Jude Fawley's first job is to scare
rooks to stop them eating the newly sown seed.

2/5 *Arabella, we are told, has the 'rich complexion of a cochin's
hen's egg'. What is a cochin?* A variety of chicken, originally from
China, mainly kept for ornamental purposes. Their eggs (of
which they lay few) are characteristically brown. The cochins
were first imported into England in 1845, and sparked off a
chicken 'gold rush'. Arabella's father, as we later gather, raises
them to sell.

2/6 *Where do the newly wed Fawleys honeymoon?* At the cottage where they will live.

2/7 *Jude has given Arabella a framed lover's photograph of himself. What happens to it?* Arabella throws it out as junk to be auctioned. Jude buys it and burns it.

2/8 *What occupation did Sue's (unlucky) father follow?* He was an ecclesiastical worker in metal in London. The religiosity has, we apprehend, burned deep into Sue's psyche, manifesting itself initially as fanatic freethinking, and latterly as religious mania.

2/9 *How old is Mr Phillotson?* When he is met again by Jude at Lumsden he is around forty-five and careworn. This means he must have been in his mid-thirties when we first encounter him at Marygreen—rather old, perhaps, to be starting an undergraduate career.

2/10 *What do Phillotson and Sue plan to do, when she has her 'certificate' from the teaching college?* They will open a double school (i.e. one for both boys and girls). The assumption is that she will not have children—at least not for some time. Presumably Phillotson is paying for her studies at college, although this detail is never confirmed.

2/11 *Why is Sue's excuse that Jude is her cousin not acceptable to her mentors at the college?* The same excuse was made (mendaciously) by a seduced fellow trainee, twelve months earlier. It led to some very wounding publicity for the institution.

2/12 *What is Phillotson's 'old-fashioned ... style of shaving'?* Presumably he has long sideburns.

2/13 *Why does Jude warn Phillotson that it is 'dangerous' for him to sit on the bare block of stone?* Because it is commonly thought to encourage piles.

2/14 *What is the name of the composer of 'The Foot of the Cross' and why, may we surmise, does Hardy introduce him?* We never know his name. He plays no significant part in the otherwise carefully constructed plot. Hardy seems to have introduced the episode as a flanking attack on the predatory publishing industry: 'These publishing people—they want the copyright of an obscure composer's work, such as mine is, for almost less than I should have to pay a person for making a fair manuscript copy of the score.' He is perhaps thinking of his personal experiences as the author of *The Poor Man and the Lady* and *Desperate Remedies* with the dubious publisher William Tinsley.

2/15 *How can the Widow Edlin, in Marygreen, 'telegraph' Jude that 'Your aunt is sinking. Come at once'?* She presumably gets a boy to send it from the railway station at Aldbrickham.

2/16 *Why does the school board at Shaston require Phillotson to resign?* For 'condoning . . . adultery'. He would presumably have been forgiven had his wife merely deserted him.

2/17 *On a number of occasions Jude calls Sue his 'comrade'. What are the overtones of the word?* Marxist, perhaps, but more probably Whitmanesque—suggesting an adventurously secular attitude towards sex rather than any disposition to world revolution.

2/18 *What is Little Father Time's baptismal Christian name?* We never know. In England, he is renamed Jude, or 'Juey', after his father. He himself seems not to know his name. In Australia, his surname may have been Donn or Cartlett. It is odd that he does not, on first appearing in the novel, have an Australian accent although, as we are told, he later picks up the Wessex dialect. There is a further mystery in why the Donns, in Australia, should go to the considerable expense of shipping the boy back to his mother in England. A cheaper alternative for an unwanted child could surely have been found where Arabella left him.

2/19 *Who is the one guest Jude invites to his (abortive) wedding,* *and why?* The Widow Edlin. She is 'the only person remaining on earth who was associated with his early life at Marygreen'.

2/20 *What great crime and punishment lurks in the background of the Fawley–Bridehead family?* As the Widow Edlin informs them, one of their ancestors was 'gibbeted just on the brow of the hill by the Brown House', for the crime of stealing his dead child from his estranged wife. 'They brought it in burglary, and that's why he was hanged and gibbeted.' It seems strange that Jude, who must have passed the spot countless times in his first twenty years, has never heard of this macabre family legend. Since the 'bloody code' was reformed (in 1829), the anecdote may possibly hint that one day divorce will be as tenderly dealt with as such cases of burglary now are.

2/21 *What pseudonyms for Oxford colleges are given in the novel?* Sarcophagus, Rubric, Cardinal, Oldgate, Biblioll.

2/22 *Sue calls herself Mrs Fawley. Does she wear a wedding ring?* It would go against the grain for Sue to wear a ring. The landlady in Christminster turns her away because of her advanced pregnancy—immediately visible. The landlady who does (temporarily) take her in has her suspicions. But since many working-class woman would pawn their rings (and, if necessary, band some black cotton round their finger) it may not be an obvious giveaway that her left hand is bare.

2/23 *What are the names of the two siblings Father Time hangs in the closet?* We never know, any more than we know the name of the pig that Jude kills or the rabbit whose neck he breaks.

2/24 *What did Arabella's 'mother' (i.e. stepmother) die of in Australia?* As she says, 'dys—'. Dysentery. Arabella would have a cruder dialect name for the disorder which she is too genteel, as a respectable married lady, to use. It is one of many hints that the pig-jobber's household is filthy.

2/25 *Why does Jude take Arabella into his lodgings at Christminster?* To prevent her going on the streets. Two undergraduates, as she says, have 'winked' at her. There was widespread and scandalous prostitution in the city for the benefit of (ostensibly) 'celibate' college men.

Level Three

3/1 *What should one read into the novel's epigraph, 'The letter killeth'?* Its primary sense would seem to be that 'the letter of the law', as opposed to its spirit, is destructive. But in Hardy's ironic view of things 'letters' (dialect for learning) kill. As one of the 'self-taught' (as he labels himself), Jude embodies an anti-Smilesian lesson (Samuel Smiles being the author of the immensely influential manual for young Victorian lads on the rise in life, *Self-Help*). Education destroys.

3/2 *In his Preface to the first edition, Hardy claims that* Jude the Obscure *is a novel 'addressed by a man to men and women of full age'. What is 'full age'?* There had been much public discussion of the 'age of consent', following W. T. Stead's publicity about the law (Stead 'bought' a young girl from the London streets, to demonstrate the iniquity of twelve as the age of consent for females). 'Full age' might, as the law relating to consent had recently been reformed, mean sixteen. More likely, Hardy was thinking of the 'age of majority', twenty-one, at which point a citizen became legally competent.

3/3 *When does Jude's working week as a labouring stonemason end?* At three o'clock on Saturday. It is at the end of his working week that he first crosses the path of Arabella. She, however, is still at work, disposing of the various parts of her father's recently slaughtered pig. The long working week renders Jude's self-education all the more heroic. Much of the early action takes place on Sunday, the only day in which Arabella, Jude, Sue, and Phillotson have the whole twenty-four hours to themselves.

3/4 *What Greek dramatist is Jude fantasizing that he will get around to reading, when Arabella shouts her first 'Hoity-toity' at him? And what does 'hoity-toity' mean?* Among other Greek playwrights the 'naughty' (and much-censored) comedian Aristophanes. 'Hoity-toity' is a jeering version of 'haughty'.

3/5 *Arabella's friends assume Jude is apprenticed. Is he?* It is not clear at this point that he is. Later we are told that he is working on half-wages until he is 'out of his time', as a mason. Which master he is apprenticed to and where the business is based we do not precisely know.

3/6 *What do we know of Arabella's past?* Her mother is dead; Arabella was for a time a barmaid at Aldbrickham. Rather confusingly, she calls her stepmother (who also dies prematurely) 'mother'. For reasons which are unclear (perhaps his financial difficulties), she is, when she first meets Jude, helping her father out with his jobbing pig and pork business.

3/7 *Did Arabella deliberately loose the piglets to run all the way home, on her first attempt to seduce Jude? And was the cochin egg a ruse?* Probably yes, and yes.

3/8 *What is the 'true illumination' that Jude ignores?* That stone-masonry ('Sermons in Stones', as Ruskin called it) is as dignified as university scholarship.

3/9 *What is Jude's favourite tipple?* Beer. He has, it seems, a very poor head for liquor and gets drunk easily. His intake (unlike that of Cartlett) is modest, although the effects are invariably disastrous. Arabella (as her dosing him prior to their second marriage indicates) is much wiser in the ways of alcohol.

3/10 *What ideal does Jude hold before himself after the university dream fades?* To be a licentiate—that is to say, a clergyman who has not had the benefit of a university education.

3/11 *Jude and Sue sleep together at the shepherd's cottage, on their ill-fated day's excursion. Do they do anything more than (literally) sleep?* No, although it is presumed that they do. Courts of law would make the same cynical presumption.

3/12 *Whose is the second photograph in Sue's cubicle (Phillotson being the first), and whose the third, which will never be there?* One is an 'undergraduate in cap and gown' (her first lover). Jude's picture will never be there, since she is expelled before having any opportunity to put it up.

3/13 *Who tells the authorities at Sue's college that Jude has been dismissed from his post for drunkenness and blasphemy?* It may well have been the curate, Highbridge, at Marygreen, to whom he confessed his delinquencies. Otherwise the usual gossip circuits have been humming.

3/14 *Does Arabella really think that Jude had died after she decamped to Australia?* Her friends at Marygreen would surely have told her were he dead (and she free). It seems that she is protecting herself against the allegation of knowingly committing the serious crime of bigamy.

3/15 *When, at Shaston, Jude—playing the eavesdropper and voyeur, as he often does—sees Sue press a photograph against her bosom, whose photograph is it? And what part do photographs play in the action?* It must be Jude's, although when he gave it to her we do not know. One assumes that, as was common in the 1860s and 1870s, he ordered a batch of *carte-de-visite*-sized pictures (presumably from a travelling photographer, who came through Marygreen). He gave one of his photographs to Arabella. She threw it out as junk on decamping to Australia (Jude bought it at auction and burned it). Later, however, Arabella reminds Cartlett, by reference to certain photographs of hers which he has seen, of what Jude looked like. Presumably she kept them to prove in Australia that she was a lawful 'widow'.

3/16 *Why does Sue say that living as she does, in intimate connection with Phillotson, is 'adultery'?* It is not easy to construct what goes on in the Phillotson bedroom. Eight weeks of marital relations are 'torture' to her—apparently because he can have her whenever he wishes. He gives her, however, 'liberty'—which elderly husbands do not always do. Do they use contraceptives? She has no children with him, although with Jude she is very fertile (as, apparently, is Arabella). The Phillotson marriage is probably what in the 1890s was called MINO—a marriage in name only.

3/17 *Which contingent in Shaston supports Phillotson, as he faces expulsion from his position at the school?* The local adulterers', cuckolds' and fornicators' club—that is, the 'fair' and 'travelling people': 'The body included two cheap-jacks, a shooting-gallery proprietor and the ladies who loaded the guns, a pair of boxing-masters, a steam-roundabout manager, two travelling broom-makers, who called themselves widows [i.e. lesbians], a gingerbread-stall keeper, a swing-boat owner, and a "test-your-strength" man'. No match for the forces of Victorian decency.

3/18 *When do Jude and Sue consummate their love relationship?* Not until after they begin their pseudo-marriage—although when she runs away from Phillotson it is assumed by the world (or the prurient folk at Aldbrickham) that they are living in sin. If the relationship with Phillotson was MINO, this is AINO—adultery in name only.

3/19 *What does it mean when Sue is described by Jude as a 'phantasmal, bodiless creature'?* She is, one might guess, a version of Keats's *belle dame sans merci*. Physiologically, we are to believe, she lacks what he later calls 'animal' characteristics. It is not, apparently, primarily physiological (i.e. a deficiency in the 'lust' department) but 'nervous'—to do with her mental and neural make-up. It is not clear whether she is a manifestation of racial degeneration (the result of too much inbreeding of intellectuals, one of the fears of 1890s' eugenicists) or the forerunner of a superior kind of human being (a eugenic ideal type).

3/20 *Does Arabella actually remarry in Australia? Is she, in that far-off country, Mrs Cartlett?* There are a number of references in the text to a 'hitch' in the Cartlett marriage (not merely the gigantic hitch of Arabella's bigamy). As would be possible in the distant colony, it may be merely a sham marriage. Possibly Cartlett was himself a married man when he met Arabella. Her leaving him, and his acquiescence in remarrying her in England seems to suggest that their union was, in its first manifestation, somewhat irregular. Arabella is, of course, the supreme pragmatist about such things.

3/21 *It has been noted that the dominant image in* Jude the Obscure *is of a hunted animal being done painfully to death. How many animal deaths are described in the novel, and who kills the beasts?* Notoriously, the pig-sticking and bleeding, which precipitates the break-up of Jude's first marriage. Jude stabs the animal savagely, to ease its terminal suffering. He also gives the rabbit caught and screaming in the wire gin its quietus by the traditional means of breaking its neck with a downward chop of the side of his hand (he has evidently done it many times before). Vilbert entices pigeons to his roof with rock salt, and kills them to make up his quack medicines. Jude and Sue have pet pigeons which are destined, on the auction of their household effects, to be bought by a local poulterer and slaughtered for the table. Sue releases them. The omen, alas, is not good. The pigeons may escape, but Jude and Sue do not.

3/22 *Who taught Arabella to write correct letters (as she manifestly does) when her speech is so richly ungrammatical?* Late in the novel, we learn that she was a pupil of Phillotson's during his brief stay at Marygreen, where he had a high reputation as a teacher. Working in a public house, it would also have been necessary for Arabella to be quick with addition (pounds, shillings, and pence were difficult to work with).

3/23 *Why, when everyone from looking at her knows that Sue is in the last stages of pregnancy, does Father Time not apprehend that she* is with child? Why does it come as such a surprise to him? ('O God, mother, you've never a-sent for another'). He has, after all, witnessed her previous two confinements. Time's blindspot is mysterious. Despite the closeness of the evidence, he does not seem to know 'the facts of life'—this seems to be the implication of her 'sending' for another as, for example, he was 'sent for' from Australia.

3/24 *Why, if he calls London London (and areas within the city like Lambeth Lambeth) does Hardy not call Christminster Oxford?* It seems odd, more so as the identification of places in Christminster (e.g. Fourways = Carfax) is so transparent. It seems a point of consistency that everywhere in Wessex must have a Wessex pseudonym.

3/25 *Why does Phillotson return to Marygreen, of all places, if he wishes to escape the scandals which have blighted his teaching career?* Presumably as a kind of masochistic self-punishment. The careers of all the characters are ironically circular.

Level Four

4/1 *In his Preface to the first edition, Hardy notes that the 'scheme' for* Jude the Obscure *was 'jotted down in 1890, from notes made in 1887'. What is the significance of these dates?* The 1890s were, self-consciously, *fin de siècle*—infused with a sense of things coming to an end. February 1887 saw the massive demonstration, nicknamed 'Bloody Sunday', in Trafalgar Square, and a sense that Britain was, under the pressure of years'-long depression (particularly in agriculture), teetering on revolution. Virginia Woolf claimed that *Jude the Obscure* is the only major novel of Hardy's that can truly be called 'pessimistic'. There would seem to be some historical justification for this mood. Personal justification, too: Hardy's cousin Tryphena Sparks (the original of Sue Bridehead, it is claimed) died in 1890.

4/2 *What is the 'missile' which Arabella throws at Jude, to get his attention?* Otherwise called a 'scrap of offal' and 'novel artillery', Arabella's parodic Cupid's dart is the 'characteristic part of a barrow-[i.e. castrated] pig': a useless penis. Arabella's later remark that it is 'nothing. It is my father's' is typically saucy.

4/3 *Is Arabella a virgin at the start of the novel?* The girl in the inn evidently has her doubts. But the way in which Arabella's friends, Anny and Sarah, put her up to the marriage trap suggests that she is 'pure'—physically, if not morally.

4/4 *Why does Arabella so want to marry Jude, why* must *she have him and no other young working-class man?* He is a comely young fellow, but her need seems to be somehow parallel to his. She sees Jude, that is, as a way of rising above her low status in life. Practically, she sees him as a stonemason who will rise in his trade—if he will only leave off the books. Her mistake may be similar to that of Eustacia Vye in marrying Clym Yeobright.

4/5 *Arabella is 'brighter' after her interview with Vilbert, after her first lovemaking with Jude. Why?* Presumably he tells her (wrongly) that she is pregnant, which gives her the necessary leverage to get Jude to the altar. Later she tells Jude that she was 'mistaken'. Alternatively, Vilbert may have reassured her that she was *not* pregnant.

4/6 *Why is Arabella, having so wanted to marry Jude, so quick to leave him?* She has found him a 'slow old coach', and she wants more out of life (as does he) than the marriage supplies. She is also, as her friends warn her, dangerously 'restless' in her affections.

4/7 *Why, given the huge significance it has had in his life, has Jude apparently never been to Christminster before arriving there at the age of twenty-two?* So unfamiliar is the place that he brings a map with him when he first arrives. It is, as we are frequently told, only twenty miles or so from Alfredston, itself only a few miles from Marygreen. Had he been there in the intervening ten years, Jude would surely have been reunited with Phillotson and have met Sue (although she has spent some time in London). This remoteness from Christminster suggests that, although imminent, the huge connectedness of Victorian Britain (largely brought about by trains, better roads, and the penny post) has still to reach deepest Wessex.

4/8 *Why is it 'not well for cousins to fall in love'?* As eugenicists would point out, inbreeding 'degenerates the racial stock'. Fear of such degeneration was something of a moral panic in the 1890s. From an eugenic point of view (and did he have the future of England in mind?), Jude would do much better to 'outbreed' with the hardy peasant, Arabella.

4/9 *Jude has a moment of truth, like Oedipus, at 'Fourways', the doom-laden crossroads in Christminster. Could he have taken a different route in life, or is his destiny preordained and immutable, like that of Sophocles' hero?* Hardy leaves the question open. The implication is always there that Jude is 'recalcitrant', or stubborn. He wants, as he later confesses, to do in one generation what can only be done, with luck, in three.

4/10 *Jude develops his passion for Sue after apparently meeting her only twice. What attracts him so immediately and fatally?* She is, we are told, the 'one affined soul' he has ever known. The relationship seems magnetic. They are, it is later said, two halves of the same person. Cynics, however, will note that he falls headlong into Arabella's love-trap. He may just be susceptible to women, as he is to drink and philosophical books.

4/11 *What does Hardy mean, when he writes of the pupils at 'the species of nunnery known as the Training-School' that all the faces bore 'the legend The Weaker' on them, which must be, 'while the inexorable laws of nature remain what they are'?* Women, it would seem, are for ever destined by the immutable laws of genetics to secondary status in Hardy's universe. Until, that is, evolution comes to the rescue.

4/12 *What do we know of the undergraduate whose picture Sue has on her wall, alongside Phillotson's?* He was a student at Christminster with whom she had a passionate affair, never consummated (frustration from which may have contributed to his premature death). We never know his name, or any details about him, other than that he left college to work as a journalist in London, cohabiting (celibately) with Sue. It was from him (the 'most irreligious man that she ever knew, and the most moral') that Sue imbibed her views about life and the relationship of the sexes. The nameless young undergraduate is, indirectly, one of the most important characters in the novel.

4/13 *How far advanced was Arabella's pregnancy, when she left for Australia?* It seems unlikely that she did not suspect she was pregnant, before she left England. Why she should have chosen even so to leave Jude is very mysterious, as mysterious as why she should have deserted her second husband in Sydney.

4/14 *Why does Aunt Drusilla tell Sue, with reference to Phillotson, 'there be certain men here and there that no woman of any niceness can stomach. I should have said he was one.' What is there about Phillotson that revolts women?* 'Niceness' is a strange word. Is there some suggestion of homosexuality—the manly friendship with Gillingham? A hint of pederasty, perhaps (why does he change jobs so frequently)? He is at some deep level repulsive, which of course makes Sue's final submission to him so horrific. Jude, by contrast, seems irresistible to 'women' (see, for example, Arabella's passionate declaration that she 'must' have him, or Sue's flying to him (and lifelong scandal), despite her best intentions as a respectably married woman).

4/15 *What is the name of the public house that Mr and Mrs (so-called) Cartlett take over in Lambeth, on their return from Australia? How is it different from, for example, the rustic inn at which*

Arabella and Jude did their courting? The Cartletts' house is the Three Horns. It is one of the new 'free, fully-licensed public' houses in Lambeth (famous for its drunkenness, hence 'The Lambeth Walk'). Being fully licensed, the Three Horns can sell spirits and is, in nineteenth-century parlance, a gin palace. The licensing laws were progressively 'reformed' throughout the late nineteenth century, to accommodate the vast expansion of the urban population. Much later, Arabella complains that the brewers leave her with nothing after her husband has drunk himself to death, which suggests that the Three Horns is not a free house, but tied to one company. Or perhaps Cartlett was obliged to sell out.

4/16 *What hitch obliges Arabella to marry Cartlett twice?* Arabella's second marital adventure, and misadventures, on the other side of the world, can only be reconstructed speculatively. It seems that she told Cartlett she was a widow—assuming, that is, he married her there, as she claims. Her leaving Australia so precipitately suggests that he found out about Father Time (and drew his own conclusions), or that Arabella's father enlightened him as to her married state. It is hard to see otherwise why she would have burned her bridges so riskily. Clearly, Cartlett, alone and without her resourceful management of his establishment, came round to forgiving her, even following her back to England.

4/17 *When Sue tells Jude that she cannot give herself to Phillotson because of 'a repugnance on my part, for a reason I cannot disclose, and what would not be admitted as one by the world in general',* what does she mean? It is somewhat mystifying. Plenty of women in the 1890s might object to the carnality of sex. Does Phillotson, perhaps, have halitosis? She gives herself willingly enough to Jude.

4/18 *'The letter killeth'—what letter(s), precisely?* Those mentioned in 3/1, but also the dismissive letter from the Master of Biblioll College. At Aldbrickham, Jude carves letters (blocked out by Sue) on headstones (for the dead). The pulmonary inflammation produced by this work—black lung, pneumo-coniosis—does, literally, kill Jude finally.

4/19 *Why does Sue jump out of the window when Phillotson blunders into her ('their') bedroom, and why does she* say *she jumps out of the window?* In a direct allusion to Rebecca, in *Ivanhoe*, who threatens to jump out of the window, rather than face violation by the savage Norman knight, Sue jumps rather than be conjugally embraced by Phillotson, who has absent-mindedly blundered into her bedroom. She claims, rather unconvincingly, that she was sleepwalking, and acting under the influence of 'a terrible dream'. None of the door locks works, she observes.

4/20 *Why does Jude, a gifted artisan we gather, not thrive in his line of work?* Having served his apprenticeship at Marygreen, Jude becomes a cathedral mason at Christminster. This would seem to be highly skilled work and, given the huge amount of decaying Christminster fabric, decently remunerative. But Jude never seems to advance. Why does he not, at least, become a foreman, manager, or even—like Michael Henchard—an owner of his own business? Later he does headstones and epitaphs, before sinking to the level of 'journeyman' or day worker (although a worker with 'guild' status). Finally, reverting to the skills taught him by his baker great-aunt, he makes gingerbread 'Christminster cakes' to be sold at fairs. Why it is he cannot advance in his trade—as the sensible Master of Biblioll College advises—is mysterious. Even his pastries seem superior articles. His career as a worker on ecclesiastical buildings is also, we assume, blighted by his 'scandalous' private life.

4/21 *What* is *Hardy's view on divorce?* This is one of the harder questions raised by the novel. Hardy's comment, in his 1912 Preface, is enigmatic on the subject: 'the famous contract—sacrament I mean—is doing fairly well still, and people marry and give in what may or may not be true marriage as light-heartedly as ever. The author has even been reproached by some earnest correspondents that he has left the question where he

found it, and has not pointed the way to a much-needed reform.'
As one reads the novel, however, it seems that the quartet of main
characters, using the legal instrument of the 1857 Act, separate
from each other remarkably easily (although Phillotson and Jude
are obliged to petition; adultery not being, by itself, admissible
grounds for the woman as for the man). The implication of the
novel is that divorce should be approved—condoned—more *gen-
erously* by society at large. Society, that is to say, should go beyond
the 'letter' of matrimonial law into the spirit of the union of man
and woman. Hardy specifically does not ally himself with radical
'New Woman' or 'anarchist' positions on the subject. Nor does he
entirely seem to approve what he calls the 'dark morality' of
sexuality. 'The Agnostics', Hardy observes, had 'scarcely been
heard of at this time'. (Since T. H. Huxley introduced the term in
1869, this would suggest, again, the 1870s as a date for the novel.)
Arabella evidently has studied the 1857 Act. When she breaks
with Jude, she very publicly (and mendaciously) displays to the
world (Marygreen, at least) 'how he's served me! . . . Making me
work Sunday mornings when I ought to be going to my church,
and tearing my hair off my head, and my gown off my back!' She
will have her witnesses, should she need them in court.

4/22 *'They are making it easier for poor students* now', *says Sue.
When, precisely, is the 'now' in the novel?* A very difficult question.
Sue's comment is one of the very few references to current
affairs, or anything that could help the reader fill in the historical
scaffolding around Jude's career (who, for example, was Prime
Minister? Does the action cross Queen Victoria's Jubilees?). We
know, of course, that the main action is set in what Hardy calls
'railway days', and that the adult Jude's is a world in which people
can communicate easily by telegram. But this could mean any
decade after the 1840s (in which decade the railway, and the
telegraph poles alongside the track, came to Wessex). As regards
higher education, in 1895, when *Jude the Obscure* was published,
it was actually harder for indigent students to enter Oxbridge,
with the opening of scholarships to all, not merely to needy can-
didates. Sue's comment quoted above would seem to refer to the

setting up of provincial universities, such as Owens College in Manchester, or the large metropolitan institutions in London. It is, however, never entirely clear when the narrative is set, or what span of the nineteenth century Jude's thirty-odd years cover. From his not being obliged to attend school at Marygreen (he is eleven when the novel opens), we assume that the first section precedes the universal education Act of 1870. At Shaston, however, with its mention of stern school inspectors and sterner governors, we assume that Phillotson is, at the brief high point of his wretched career, the principal of a post-1870 school. There is no mention in the novel of any of the 'New Woman' (or Girton Girl) agitation which was something of a vogue in the 1890s. Jude's and Sue's reading seems locked in the 1870s, with Swinburne being the most recent author mentioned by them. Since both of them are bookish, it seems odd that they would not, were the novel set in the 1890s, have come across some of the more progressive thinking on such matters as female emancipation, divorce, and 'open unions'. Sue seems to be a 'New Woman' *avant la lettre*. Hardy, in fact, seems to boast of the fact in his 1912 Preface, where he states: 'an experienced reviewer . . . informed the writer that Sue Bridehead, the heroine, was the first delineation in fiction of the woman who was coming into notice in her thousands every year—the woman of the feminist movement—the slight, pale "bachelor" girl—the intellectualized, emancipated bundle of nerves that modern conditions were producing' (as a matter of literary history, that credit usually goes to Grant Allen's *The Woman Who Did*, 1895; Herminia Barton—the 'woman' of the title—comes to an even more painful end than Sue). In the same Preface, Hardy alludes to 'the difficulties down to twenty or thirty years back of acquiring knowledge in letters without pecuniary means'. This would suggest that Jude was born, say, in 1860 and died in 1894. The agricultural depressions of the early 1880s would also account for the Donns' emigration to Australia, with the collapse of the pig trade in Wessex. But arguably the historical vagueness against which the novel's vivid narative is set was intended by Hardy as conscious artistic impressionism (as it often is with his disciple, D. H. Lawrence).

4/23 *What is the arc of Jude's professional life?* He begins as a rook-scarer and drawer of water. He works in his great-aunt's bakery. He becomes an apprentice stonemason around Marygreen. He becomes a cathedral mason in Christminster—the apogee of his career. He descends, at Aldbrickham, to an engraver of head-stones and a maker of epitaphs. He works thereafter, following his marital disgrace, as a journeyman (day worker). Finally, he bakes 'monumental' Christminster cakes, for sale at markets and fairs. During his second marriage to Arabella, he picks up some casual masonry work at Christminster, repairing the fabric of colleges 'he could never enter'—but is too ill to do much in that way.

4/24 *Why do Sue and Jude not practise contraception?* This is one of the mysteries of the Fawley bedroom. Sue has two children in quick succession, and is pregnant with a third when the holocaust precipitated by Father Time wipes out the younger generation of the family. She, at least, would know about contraception (even Vilbert has what are evidently effective remedies against unwanted little strangers). When Sue finally surrenders to Phillotson she does not, as far as we know, conceive (nor did she during the eight bitter honeymoon months). It seems, if anything, an indica-tion of the 'erotolepsy'—or sexual recklessness—of Jude and Sue. Contraception of various kinds (condom, douche, prophy-lactic sponge) was available to the middle classes from the 1870s onwards. Had Time not practised his own brand of family plan-ning ('Done because we are too meny') how many offspring would the Fawleys have had?

4/25 *What does Esther do with her hair?* In the disturbing epi-graph to 'At Christminster Again', Hardy quotes from the apoc-ryphal Book of Esther: '. . . And she humbled her body greatly, and all the places of her joy she filled with her torn hair.' It is one of the more horrible allusions in the novel, reflecting on Sue's abasement.

The Oxford World's Classics Website

www.worldsclassics.co.uk

- Information about new titles
- Explore the full range of Oxford World's Classics
- Links to other literary sites and the main OUP webpage
- Imaginative competitions, with bookish prizes
- Peruse the Oxford World's Classics Magazine
- Articles by editors
- Extracts from Introductions
- A forum for discussion and feedback on the series
- Special information for teachers and lecturers

www.worldsclassics.co.uk

American Literature

British and Irish Literature

Children's Literature

Classics and Ancient Literature

Colonial Literature

Eastern Literature

European Literature

History

Medieval Literature

Oxford English Drama

Poetry

Philosophy

Politics

Religion

The Oxford Shakespeare